CYCLING IN NOTTINGHAMSHIRE

Penny & Bill Howe

Published by Sigma Leisure – an imprint of
Sigma Press, 1 South Oak Lane, Wilmslow, Cheshire SK9 6AR, England.

British Library Cataloguing in Publication Data
A CIP record for this book is available from the British Library.

ISBN: 1-85058-443-5

Typesetting and Design by: Sigma Press, Wilmslow, Cheshire.

Cover photograph: Cycling in Sherwood Forest
(Tim Hughes/Cyclographics Publications)

Maps and photographs: the authors

Printed by: Manchester Free Press

Disclaimer: the information in this book is given in good faith and is believed to be correct at the time of publication. No responsibility is accepted by either the author or publisher for errors or omissions, or for any loss or injury howsoever caused. Only you can judge your own fitness, competence and experience.

Contents

Introduction

The home of Robin Hood 1
The Rides 2
What kind of bike? 3
Maps and Guides 3
Cycle Notes
    Food and fitness 4
    Clothing and equipment 5
    Getting to the rides 6
    British Rail 6
    General information 7
Key to maps 10

The Rides

1. The Major Oak 11
10 miles

2. Sherwood Pines Forest Trail, Clipstone Forest 15
7 miles or 15 miles

3. Laxton to Ossington 20
9.5 miles

4. Laxton to Ompton 23
10 miles

5. Clumber Park. Short Ride 27
6.5 miles

6. Clumber Park. Corunna Lodge 31
13 miles

7. Creswell Crags Ride 36
6 miles

8. Welbeck Abbey   **39**
13 miles

9. Southwell to Farnsfield   **46**
11 miles or 16 miles

10. Southwell to Thurgarton   **51**
15 miles

11. Eakring   **55**
10.5 miles

12. Beauvale   **60**
4.5 miles

13. Haggs Farm   **63**
6.5 miles

14. Cossall   **66**
5 miles

15. Blidworth & Papplewick Pumping station   **71**
8 miles

16. Epperstone & Lambley   **75**
12.5 miles

17. Kneesall   **80**
9 miles

18. Winkburn   **83**
10 miles

19. Blyth   **86**
14 miles

20. Pleasley Trails – Part 1   **91**
10 miles

21. Pleasley Trails – Part 2   **95**
3.75 miles

22. Thrumpton Road Ride   **98**
15 miles

23. Thrumpton Off-road Ride   **103**
11 miles

24. East Markham   **109**
11 miles

25. Bothamsall Off-road   **115**
13.5 miles

26. Colston Bassett On-road Ride   **120**
19 miles

27. Colston Bassett Off-Road Ride   **124**
15 miles

28. Flintham   **128**
12 miles or 13 miles

29. Car Colston   **132**
10 miles

30. Stanton on the Wolds   **136**
12 miles

31. Bunny – Home of the Wrestling Baronet   **139**
10 miles

32. Newark to Nottingham – south of the Trent Valley   **143**
25.5 miles

33. Nottingham to Newark – north of the Trent Valley   **150**
25 miles

34. Retford to West Stockwith & the Chesterfield Canal   **159**
16 miles

35. River Idle, West Stockwith to Retford   **165**
24 miles plus 3-mile diversion

36. Clumber Park to Lincoln   **171**
32 miles

TOWN & VILLAGE INDEX   **179**

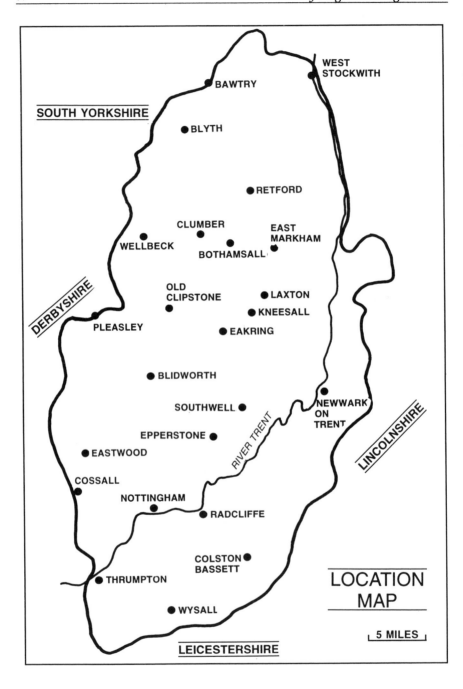

Nottinghamshire

The home of Robin Hood

Nottinghamshire is a land of hills and dales, of forests and moorland, of remote sparsely populated rural communities and close-packed mining villages. It has a great deal of variety to offer both the modern day explorer and the amateur historian, as well as those just seeking beautiful, quiet routes for cycling. It stretches about fifty miles from its border with Yorkshire in the north, to Leicestershire in the south, and nearly thirty miles from the fenland border with Lincolnshire in the east to the foothills of the Derbyshire Pennines in the west. Two major historical travellers' routes pass through the south of the county, the Fosse Way, the Roman Road from the West Country to Lincoln, and the River Trent which gave access to the very heart of England to both traders and invaders for centuries, and which also forms much of the eastern boundary of the county as it wends its way north to the Humber and the North Sea.

North of these two great arteries are the remains of Sherwood Forest, which probably covered nearly a fifth of the county in the days when the hunting was reserved for the king. The soil here is generally of poor quality and shallow, as evidenced by the abundant silver birches, and in the past was unsuitable for farming, though modern methods have enabled agriculture to encroach on the old forest. Modern industry and coal mining have stolen more of the forest and heathland yet there are still many leafy rides where the only companions you may have are the birds and the beasts of the forest as your cycle wheels roll through the leaf mould of centuries.

Much of Nottinghamshire's industry is now defunct and the old buildings, such as mills, are becoming part of our industrial heritage. The great grey spoil tips of the coal fields are disappearing under a cloth of green as the county seeks a new image and a new future in the aftermath of the collapse of the coal industry. Perhaps what is needed is a modern day Robin Hood, to emulate that legendary figure known the world over as a champion of ordinary people.

Those intrigued by myth and legend will find plenty to interest them around the county which also contains the site of one of the countries few jousting fields. The dividing line between myth and legend may be rather blurred at times, as at East Stoke where a woodland gully has become known as Red Gutter, reputedly the place where a large army was slaughtered. Or is it only named after the redwood trees that grow in the gully?

The county was torn asunder at the time of the Civil War with neighbouring villages and estates supporting different sides, friends becoming enemies, country houses made into fortified retreats. On a more peaceful note the county was the ancestral home of many of the people who became known as The Pilgrim Fathers, of the Quaker George Fox, and of the Methodists John and Charles Wesley.

One of the most striking things about the county is the abundance of beautiful gardens. From miners' cottages to mansions, in town and country, even the allotments seem extraordinarily productive. It comes as no surprise to find that Nottinghamshire is the home of 'The Rose King' Samuel Hole, influential in the founding of the National Rose Society.

Samuel's nickname was given to him by Tennyson, which leads us towards the county's literary connections. D.H. Lawrence was born at Eastwood and used many places in that area in his books. Byron inherited Newstead Abbey, and the title of 6th Lord Byron, at the age of ten. Alan Sillitoe was born in Nottingham, Kate Greenaway spent her childhood holidays in Rolleston, and many more notable literary figures lived and worked in the county.

The county abounds in waterways both natural and man-made and fishing is an extremely popular past-time. But many waterways are also navigable and the colourful narrow-boat can be seen chugging almost silently along beside some of the routes in this book. The waterways are also home to many native birds and temporary home to visiting species. The abundance of forests both large and small means that not only birds but many animals from badgers to deer can be spotted by those with the patience to wait and watch.

Nottinghamshire has so much to offer and, whatever your hobby, the best way to travel is by bicycle which not only improves your fitness and health but makes you independent of modern polluting forms of transport.

The Rides

These rides have been devised with mixed ability groups in mind and are intended to give the rider time to make their own discoveries or pursue their own hobbies. The experienced cyclist will probably combine two or more rides to make a more testing ride. They are almost all circular rides, apart from a few that are half of a two-day circular ride and one that takes the rider into the neighbouring county of Lincolnshire. The routes mostly follow minor roads and quiet country lanes, bridle-paths and tracks, with an occasional bit on a major road where there is no alternative. Where possible we have mentioned the presence of a footway beside major roads, but remember that it is illegal to cycle on the pavement.

The average length of the rides is quite short as the county of Nottinghamshire is rather hilly and a long ride could be an exhausting experience with a couple of youngsters in the party. To compensate, the county has some of the most beautiful off-road riding in the country. The forest tracks are mostly a dream to ride, though it is still possible to find some really taxing off-road routes for serious mountain bikers. The condition of bridle-paths and tracks can change with time and the seasons, a particularly wet winter can create a mire that will take months to clear, while a long dry summer can leave good paths dangerously cracked. The countryside is an ever-changing canvas with each season bringing a fresh delight to the eye. Your view may well be unique, cherish it.

What kind of bike?

These rides are intended to be suitable for any kind of bike, from Gran's old shopper to junior's high-tech mountain bike, though some of the roughest routes may be uncomfortable on a really narrow-tyred racer. If you are going to buy a bike take as much advice from regular cyclists as you can, join the C.T.C. and ask the technical department for advice. There are also some good cycle shops around.

Today, the whole family, from grandparents to toddlers can take to the road. Child seats and baby trailers enable housebound mothers to get out and about again. You can still buy tandems, but there are devices to adapt two ordinary bikes into a temporary tandem, or to attach half a child-sized bike to the rear of almost any adult bike.

Maps and Guides

The maps accompanying each ride in this book are intended only as a guide. We recommend the use of the relevant Ordnance Survey maps to enable you to discover even more of interest on each route. The most useful series is the Landranger 1:50,000. If you require greater detail, the Pathfinder 1:25,000 series is excellent.

There are many guides to Britain's flora and fauna, but we use the compact Collins Gem Guides which cover many subjects, including wild flowers, birds and butterflies.

There are several cycle route guides available for cyclists in the county, some of which are free. Ask specifically for these, and a list of those to buy, when contacting the Tourist Office. Ask also for leaflets aimed at equestrians if you are interested in off-road riding.

Cycle Notes

Cycling is one of the most pleasant ways of keeping fit and healthy as it can be combined with so many other interests. Even gentle cycling will increase your fitness, but if you are really trying to lose weight you will need to do more than potter out for an afternoon ride. Spending at least one mile of each ride and stretching yourself to the limit (not on that easy downhill stretch!) will really help to tone up the muscles and fight the flab.

Food

Food is the only fuel required by a cyclist. You use considerable energy while cycling and your body needs plenty of complex carbohydrates, which are released slowly into the bloodstream, to enable it to keep the wheels turning. Included in this category are: muesli; porridge; bread (preferably whole-meal); pasta; homemade cakes. Avoid fatty and/or sugary foods and fizzy drinks.

Cyclists should drink plenty of non-alcoholic, non-fizzy, fluid, especially on windy days when sweat evaporates unnoticed and fluid levels can drop alarmingly (alcohol dehydrates and should be avoided). The best drink is water, but unsweetened fruit juices are good too. On long journeys, try our version of Arabic Tea: weak tea (half the amount of tea you usually use) with a little dried or fresh mint or sage, and perhaps a squeeze of lemon juice.

Fit for the road

Whichever bike you have it must be fit for the road. However old the bike the frame and wheels must be sound and are best checked by an expert. Brake and gear cables are extremely important and should be renewed if the bike has been unused for long. For those flummoxed by terms such as bottom brackets, head stems, or multi-ratio clusters, a good cycle shop is the answer. But if your interest in one of the world's simplest machines is aroused, there is great fun to be had by getting your hands dirty and 'doing it yourself' with the help of a good cycle maintenance book.

A well-maintained bike is a dream to ride, while a squeaking rusty old heap is not only dangerous but also damned hard work. Don't forget to check all nuts and bolts before and after going off-road. Remember that good lights are not only sensible but also required by law if cycling at night.

A basic tool kit should be an essential part of your equipment. Carry tools and Allen keys to fit each nut and bolt, and screw. Sod's Law says the one you leave behind will be the one you need. You should always carry:

☐ A small adjustable spanner

☐ A few spare inner tubes and a puncture repair kit.

☐ Tyre levers and pump

☐ Spare light bulbs

Clothing

There has been a revolution in the outdoor clothing industry since we first kitted ourselves out. Today brilliant colours and skin-tight fashions are the order of the day and are readily available in the high street. Day-glow colours help to make us more visible but these fashionable clothes are not essential to an enjoyable ride.

The most important item of clothing is underwear: prominent seams can leave a tender part of your anatomy raw after a day in the saddle.

Common sense should prevail regarding outer clothing. In cooler weather we use lambswool sweaters but the modern fleeces are also excellent. Waterproofs are a major problem even with modern breathable fabrics, because cyclists create far more heat than walkers. A cape is a good idea as the body heat can escape easily, but it can act as a sail when the wind is blowing. Great if it's blowing the way you wish to go, hell if not!

Footware is equally important as you may wish to walk up steep hills or spend an afternoon sight-seeing. Specialist cycling shoes are not normally worn by the casual cyclist and comfortable trainers are perfectly acceptable.

Helmets

We were bare-headed cyclists at first but have both had accidents (not involving vehicles) where a helmet would have saved split skulls. Now we wear them all the time. A helmet will rarely save you from serious injury if involved in an accident with a vehicle. But a good helmet will protect your head in less serious accidents from cuts, grazes, and bumps. The best prevention is to ride with great care and follow the Highway Code.

Panniers

There are panniers available for almost any purpose, from carrying your tool kit, to valuable camera equipment, or the week's shopping from the super-market. They are rarely as waterproof as the manufacturers claim and best lined with a bin liner if carrying clothes. A bar bag is a very useful item for carrying valuables, as it converts to a shoulder bag and is easily removed from the bike.

Getting to the rides

There are three possible ways to reach the start of a ride. One way is to cycle. The second is the family car, and there are so many excellent roof and rear racks available today for carrying up to four bikes at a time; if you are cycling alone, the easiest solution is to remove the front wheel and pop the bike in the back of the car! The third and seemingly most sensible option is British Rail – trains and bikes are made for each other, as both are more environ-mentally friendly than the car.

British Rail

British Rail's attitude towards cyclists is incomprehensible. Many trains do not carry bikes at all, while on some you can book your bike. The rules and regulations are extremely complicated and if, like us, you find this ridicu-lous, letters of complaint should be sent to: Managing Director Regional Railways, Euston House, 24 Eversholt Street, P.O. Box 100, London, NW1 1DZ; The Secretary, Transport Users Consultative Committee for Eastern England, Midgate House, Midgate, Peterborough, PE1 1TN. Copies should also be sent to your local Councillors, your M.P., and the Tourist Board.

Words of advice . . .

☐ **Fords** – Though great fun, beware – slime-covered cobbles are treach-erous.

☐ **Bridleway signs** – Often well-concealed. Be observant, check your map frequently and don't just 'hope' you've got it right.

☐ **Fishermen** – Do not upset them. Fishing is one of the most popular British sports, so the best way of handling this dedicated band of 'thinkers' is to admire their tackle, patience, and skill. And never ride over their equipment.

☐ **Walkers** -- when you see them, give a warning of some kind. Ring your bell or shout. Be always the first one to move off the path, remembering that walkers have been instrumental in keeping the bridleways open for all of us.

- [ ] **No Through Roads** – Do not be put off. Where used in these routes there is always a way out for cyclists.

- [ ] **Horses** – They have been cantering along bridle-paths for centuries. Keep your eyes 'peeled' and your ears 'open'. If you frighten a horse, you will come off worst. Keep still as they pass, do not wave your arms about and speak gently.

- [ ] **Bulls** – It is a commonly held belief that it is illegal for a farmer to put a bull in a field that has a Right of Way through it. This is not true. Young bulls, up to ten months, are allowed in these fields, and any beef breed of bull that is accompanied by a herd of cows. All dairy bulls, with or without their lady friends, and all unaccompanied bulls are banned. Our experience of all cattle is that they are inquisitive animals, highly excited by two things: windy weather and dogs. Normally, they will completely ignore a cyclist passing through their field. Just make sure you give them a wide berth and don't shout or wave your arms about.

- [ ] **Cemeteries and Churchyards** – You may be forgiven for thinking we have a morbid fascination in the 'hereafter'. Not so. But we have found peace and tranquillity (plus a great deal of local history) abound in these final resting places. They provide refills for our water bottles, shade for our picnics, and many an ample porch has sheltered us from winter's chill. All this and good company too!

- [ ] **Camping** – Join the Camping and Caravanning Club and save your subscription in just two or three weekends. Details from: The Camping and Caravanning Club, Greenfields House, Westwood Way, Coventry, CV4 8JH. Tel. 01203 694995.

- [ ] **Reporting problems** – Don't just grumble about destruction or obstruction of paths, pot holes or dangerous drain covers, etc. Contact the County Council and report the problem. Something MIGHT be done about it!

Tourist Offices

Tourist Information Centres telephone numbers appear with each ride but to avoid repeating the information the full addresses appear here together with some other useful addresses. Do ask for the Rural Rides leaflet when contacting the Tourist Office.

Newark: Gilstrap Centre, Castlegate, Newark, Nottinghamshire, NG24 1BG. Tel. 01636 78962

Nottingham: 1 – 4 Smithy Row, Nottingham, NG1 2BY. Tel. 0115 9470661

Retford: Amcott House, Grove Street, Retford, Nottinghamshire, DN22 6JU. Tel. 01777 860780

Sherwood Forest: Sherwood Forest Visitor Centre, Edwinstowe, near Mansfield, Nottinghamshire, NG21 9HN. Tel. 01623 824490/823202

Ollerton: Sherwood Heath, Ollerton Roundabout, Ollerton, Newark, Nottinghamshire, NG22 9DR. Tel. 01623 824545

West Bridgford: County Hall, Loughborough Road, West Bridgford, Nottingham, NG2 7QP. Tel. 0115 9773558

Worksop: Public Library, Memorial Avenue, Worksop, Nottinghamshire, S80 2BP. Tel. 01909 501148

Trowell: Granada Services, M1 Northbound, 125/126 Trowell, Nottinghamshire, NG9 3PL. Tel. 0115 9442411

Nottinghamshire County Council: Leisure Services/Tourism, Trent Bridge House, Fox Road, West Bridgford, Nottingham, NG2 6BJ. Tel. 0115 9774212 (24 hours)

Nottingham City Council: Leisure & Community Services, Tourism Section, Castle Gate House, 24-30 Castle Gate, Nottingham, NG1 7AT. Tel. 0115 9483500.

Cycling clubs

For those who simply cycle for pleasure, the Cyclists Touring Club has a great deal to offer. Established in 1878, the C.T.C. exists to help cyclists of all ages and abilities, and to promote cycling as a form of transport and travel. It is the only National organisation to offer a comprehensive range of services to cyclists. These range from cycling holidays, free legal aid and Third Party insurance, to how to fix your bottom bracket! The club has 40,000 members, with local district clubs in most areas. To apply for membership, write or phone: C.T.C., Cotterell House, 69 Meadrow, Godalming, Surrey, GU7 3HS. Tel. 01483 417217.

There are several other organisations which may be of interest to cyclists: The British Mountain Bike Federation (BMBF): the governing body for both sport and recreational mountain biking with 170 affiliated clubs. Tel. 01536 412211.

The British Cycling Federation: the governing body for cycle sport. There are 1,000 local clubs and 17,000 members. Tel. 01536 412211.

The Tandem Club: 25 Hendred Way, Abingdon, Oxon, OX14 2AN.

The Veteran Cycle Club: Hyde Bank, Doctors Commons Road, Berkhamstead, HP4 3DR.

There are also several organisations which arrange rides, some for charity. For details contact:
Bike 1, Tel. 01252 624022
Bike Events, Tel. 01225 310859
Open Air, Tel. Bristol 0117 9227768

The following are groups involved with Nottinghamshire's Rural Rides Scheme who actively campaign for more attractive conditions for cyclists in the county.
Pedals: Sarah Gill, Secretary, 9 Chaworth Road, West Bridgford, Nottingham, NG2 7AE.
Pedals Nottingham North: Robin Schoolar, Secretary, 45 Morley Avenue, Mapperley, Nottingham, NG3 5FZ. Tel. 0115 9606207
Mansfield Pedals 94: Mrs Ann Jackson, Campaign Organiser, 85 Kirkby Road, Sutton in Ashfield, Nottinghamshire, Tel. 01623 512814

Follow the Cyclist's Country Code:

☐ Take nothing but photos.
☐ Leave nothing but wheel tracks.
☐ Take your litter home.
☐ Enjoy the countryside and respect its life and work.
☐ Guard against all risk of fire.
☐ Fasten all gates.
☐ Keep to Rights of Way.
☐ Leave livestock, crops, and machinery alone.
☐ Help to keep all water clean.
☐ Protect wildlife, plants, and trees.
☐ Take special care on country roads.
☐ Make no unnecessary noise.
☐ Be polite and considerate to all you meet and try to be the first to give way.
☐ Remember that cyclists are allowed on Bridleways and Public Byways, but not allowed to cycle on footpaths.
☐ Have fun!

Key to maps

A road	———————
B road	—————
Route on roads	————————→
Dangerous traffic	⚠
Tracks & RUPPs	—·—·—·—·—
Bridle-path	— — — — —
Footpath	- - - - - - - -
Railway	STATION L.C. ∕ LEVEL CROSSING •┼┼┼┼┼┼┼┼┼┼┼┼
River/Canal/Drain	〜〜〜
Pond/Lake	⬭
Bridge	⌣⌢
Church	⛪
Historic building	⬆
Windmill	⌂
Castle	ᗪᑌ
Public House	**P.H.**
Site of interest	✛
Gardens open to the public	❁
Trees	❀ ⋀
Picnic area	⛱
Campsite	⛺
Car park	Ⓟ
Golf Course	⚑

1. The Major Oak

Distance:	10 miles
Route:	Sherwood Forest Caravan Park – Birklands – Edwinstowe – Old Clipstone – Caravan Park.
Surface:	Compacted stone tracks, hard forest tracks, tarmac.
Start:	Sherwood Forest Caravan Park (SK590651)
Map:	O.S. Landranger 120 & Forest Walks in Sherwood from Forest Enterprise, Tel. 01623 822447
Parking:	If not camping there is excellent parking at Sherwood Forest Country Park on the B6034 north of Edwinstowe (SK627676). The ride would then by-pass the caravan park. There is also an unofficial pull-off beside the A6075. Coming from the west towards Ollerton, just after passing the B6035 to Warsop, the pull-off is on the left.
Accommodation:	Sherwood Forest Caravan Park, Tel. 01623 823132; an excellent site with very helpful staff. There is a wide selection of accommodation available in Edwinstowe, from B&B to hotels, contact Sherwood Forest Visitor Centre, Tel. 01623 824490/823202 for details.
Comment:	This is a pleasant ride through a leafy oak forest with the only hills right at the end of the ride on the return to the caravan site. There are recommended routes through this forest but you are allowed to ride on any forest road and hard tracks (though not on signed footpaths). This forest is very popular and best avoided during peak holiday times.

The Journey

From the reception area of the caravan park, continue round the one-way system to the T-junction, turn left and continue through the park to the white gate at the end of the road. Through the gate turn right onto the farm track that will take you up the hill and past Lamb Pens Farm, which is open to the public and has many rare breeds (reduced entry fee if staying at the caravan site). On reaching the tarmac road cross straight over to a narrow path, and go through a small patch of woodland to the A6075. Cross straight over, taking great care as this is a busy road. Opposite is the unofficial pull-off in front of large and padlocked gates into Birklands Forest. To the right of the gate is a narrow entrance and to the left is a low log barrier, both easy to negotiate.

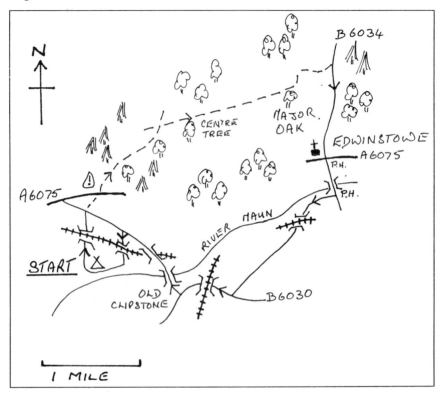

Once into the forest, you are on a wide track. Many tracks in this forest were created by the Dukes of Portland when this was their own private pleasure park in the 19th century. Pass a junction with two other tracks on your right, and continue to an obvious crossroads, turn right onto a long open sweep of carriageway. Here you have joined the Robin Hood Way and the route continues straight ahead over two forest crossroads. On your right at the second is the Centre Oak, a mighty tree which will seem small after you have seen the Major Oak. At this junction you also cross a bridle-path. If you were to turn right it would take you directly to Edwinstowe, shortening the ride, to the left it heads for the northern boundary of the forest, lengthening the ride. Either way you would miss the Major Oak, so continue straight on until the path becomes 'Walkers Only'. Dismount and follow the path to the right to the clearing where one of the mightiest trees in the country stands.

Many people think this is the tree where Robin Hood and his Merry Men met, but as the tree is thought to be only about 500 years old, it is unlikely. However, it may have grown from an acorn that fell from Robin Hood's tree! It is probable that there has always been a great oak in this part of the forest, a forest that in 1609 reputedly included 21,000 oak trees. The tree would be a convenient meeting place especially for clandestine activities, but also for people from neighbouring parishes to meet together on neutral ground for pleasure or sporting events such as cock fighting. Today the spreading branches of this gigantic tree are supported by sturdy timbers and metal ropes and visitors are kept at a respectful distance. This is a good place for a short rest before returning to the ride.

The Major Oak

Take the path that indicates '15 minute walk to the Visitor Centre', retracing your steps to the edge of the clearing and the path you entered by, then turning right. There are a couple of interesting information boards along here and some magnificent old oaks. When this main path bends sharp right, continue on a red shale vehicle track with a grass strip down the middle. From here you can cycle again and the track will take you out to a narrow opening beside a gate onto the B6034. As this is an approach road to the Visitor Centre it may be busy, take care.

Sherwood Forest Country Park Visitor Centre is on the right. There are refreshments, toilets, information areas, plenty of parking and picnicking areas. Take care crossing the road into the car park then follow the signed paths. At first follow signs to the Fairground, and the Cricket Pitch. then pass to the left of the Cricket Pitch following signs for Edwinstowe. When the path ends turn left onto the road and immediately right onto the B6034 and into the village. On your right is the church of St Mary where Robin Hood is reputed to have married Maid Marion. This church is mentioned in the Domesday Book and the tower is 700 years old. Note the variety of gargoyles. There is also a literary link with the grave of Dr Cobham Brewer, who died in 1897, and was the author of "Dictionary of Phrase and Fable" and "Reader's Handbook to Literature".

Cross straight over the A6075 at traffic lights. Here are a variety of shops including restaurants and Inns. Continue down this main street of the village, cross over the River Maun and immediately turn right into Mill Lane. The lane passes under a railway bridge then climbs through open farmland with wide views to either side. Turn right onto the B6030 at the T-junction; for a short diversion take the small lane on the left, just a little way down the hill, which leads to the remains of King John's Palace. This building is believed to have been built by the kings of Northumbria long before King John used it as a hunting lodge in the 13th century. In 1194 Richard the Lion Heart met William the Lion of Scotland here and, in 1290, Edward I held a parliament here. The building was in a state of decay by the middle of the 15th century and if you read the leaflet from the caravan site you will see that stone from the palace was used to create a unique system of flood meadows where the campsite now stands.

Return to the B6030 and continue downhill into Old Clipstone. Turn right on a nasty bend, signposted to Warsop and Caravan Site. Continue along the road which climbs through the appropriately named Gorsethorpe, no more than a couple of homesteads. Turn left into the main entrance to the caravan site. If not camping, continue to the entrance to Lamb Pens Farm and pick up the start of the route on the right.

2. Sherwood Pines Forest Trail, Clipstone Forest

Distance: Forest trail 7 miles; 15 miles circular ride from camp site.

Route: Old Clipstone – Clipstone Forest – Old Clipstone.

Surface: Tarmac; good farm tracks; Forest trails varying from deep soft sand to good hard stone.

Start: Sherwood Forest Caravan Park (SK590652)

Maps: O.S. Landranger 120 & two Forest Enterprise free leaflets (Tel. 01623 822447): 1. Forest Walks in Sherwood; 2. Cycling in the forest.

Parking: The forest has two good car parks on the cycle route.

Accommodation: The Sherwood Forest Caravan Park is an excellent site on the River Maun with a network of private trails for walkers and cyclists. Tel. 01623 823132 for details. There is also a selection of accommodation in the village of Edwinstowe and a Center Parc Village close to the forest. For information, see telephone numbers below.

Comment: Camping at Sherwood Forest Caravan Park gives easy access to this ride, and discounted admission to Sherwood Forest Farm Park with its many rare breeds. There is a steepish climb out of the campsite and some smaller hills in the forest where a few of the tracks are deep sand. The trails are very popular but the park is open from 8am to 8pm and the best times to be there are early or late when the tracks are quiet and you may catch a glimpse of some of the wild animals. This ride uses the way-marked cycle trail through the forest, but you can cycle on other forest roads. We recommend carrying a compass (and knowing how to use it) in all forest areas. For details on the area contact Sherwood Forest Visitor Centre, Tel. 01623 824490/823202; or Nottinghamshire County Council Tourism Dept., Tel. 0115 981 6898.

The Journey

For those staying at the caravan site the route begins at the reception office, continues around the one-way system and turns left at the T-junction continuing through the park between the areas named Lime, Sycamore, Larch, and Elm, etc. to a white gate at the west end of the park. Through the

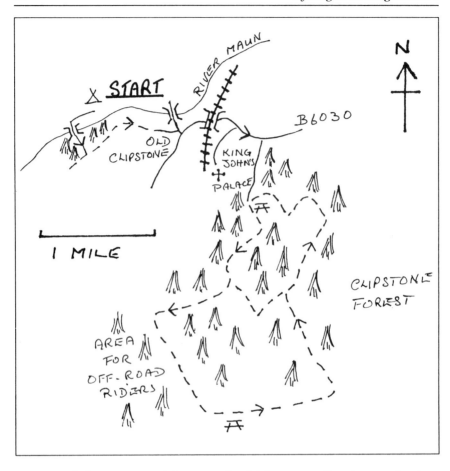

gate turn left onto a good farm track which crosses the river and enters
Cavendish wood. The track is quite steep. Continue to a junction of five
tracks. Ignore the one from the right and take the right-hand one of the three
that continue up the hill. Near the top of the hill this track has been
re-surfaced with white limestone. At the top is a T-junction, turn left and
continue with the wood on your left and open farmland beyond the hedge
on your right.

Keep straight ahead, passing a large red brick barn on your left. Note the
old farm carts stored in the open fronted barn (and the large kennel and
guard dog!). Behind the barn is the caravan site riding stables. The track
turns right onto tarmac in front of Cavendish Lodge. This is a narrow lane
that drops downhill then climbs again to Old Clipstone. Go right onto the

minor road from Gorsethorpe then left onto the B6030. Continue through the village, under the railway bridge, pass The Dog and Duck on your right and continue up the hill. The entrance to Clipstone Forest is on the right on a left-hand bend. Take care, as visibility is poor. Cross into the Forest.

This is a wide road with quite a camber, which in parts is deep cinders/broken tarmac, take great care. Follow the signs for the car park and information. For those not staying at the caravan site the journey starts at the forest car park. From the car park follow the signs to the toilets, the trail begins to the left of the toilet block. The forest had a smart information centre in this area but, just as the building was finished, vandals burned it to the ground. They hope to rebuild it by 1996. There is a refreshment stall and an unusual children's play area where all the equipment looks like creatures from the forest. The staff who maintain the park are extremely helpful, the facilities are excellent and the cycle trail is one of the best signposted we have ever ridden.

The trail begins to the left of the toilet block – closed during our visit as a swarm of bees had taken up residence! The start of the trail is marked by a large solid post, about three feet high and painted red, with a white bicycle on a green background. The trail runs south east through the pine trees on a packed-dirt path softened with pine needles. A right turn, clearly signed, takes us towards the forest nursery on an increasingly sandy track. Watch out at track junctions, if there is no signpost continue straight on.

By the nursery area the route turns left, climbing a short hill then dropping down the far side to a choice of routes. The short route continues straight on but the full 6 mile route turns right, and immediately the surface improves from treacherously sandy to hard compacted stone and the cycling improves. The route now continues straight ahead to the most western reaches of the forest, crossing several other major tracks and passing through a variety of habitats. If you really wish to see some of the forest's wild life such as the fallow deer, you will probably need to take a side track and spend some time sitting quietly.

When the route makes a sharp left turn you have reached the area set aside for off-road cyclists. Once you have turned left the route continues south but the woodland to your right is available for some exciting off-road diversions. Staying with the main route it eventually drops down a steep short hill, passes a gate, crosses another track, past another gate, then climbs another hill. The gaps beside these gates are quite narrow, not intended for loaded tourists. You soon pass out of the trees to more open heathland before dropping down to a junction of several tracks and climbing another hill that bends to the left and takes you along the southern-most edge of the forest. Soon you will reach a conveniently-placed picnic table on your right. This is roughly the halfway mark and a good place to stop for a rest. At present the viewing possibilities are good over the surrounding area, but conditions all around the forest change from year to year as small trees grow, and tall ones are felled.

The route along the southern boundary of the park is undulating but a good surface. When open farmland appears ahead the track turns left and shortly reaches a car park and a short stretch of tarmac. Pass to the right of the car park, turn left onto the tarmac, then right onto a sandy track. This is another long straight stretch which crosses several other tracks before it turns right onto quite a narrow track. At this point the short route rejoins the long route and you may meet other cyclists. We have only ridden this route early in the day and only met an occasional walker, a couple of equestrians, and a few foresters.

Sherwood Pines Forest Trail, Clipstone

On the next left turn of the route the Center Parc Village is on your right. From here there are several short sections between turnings, first left, then right, then left again, all clearly signposted as are all the other turnings. Then you are back at the start.

To return to the caravan park, follow the exit signs; it is a long-winded exit from the park but safer than going against the traffic. Take care cycling down to the road, remember the loose gravel, it can do horrendous things to bare knees! Turn left onto the B6030, down the hill, under the railway, into the village of Old Clipstone. Turn right, signposted to Warsop and Caravan Site. This turning is quite dangerous as it is impossible to see approaching traffic. The road bends right almost immediately, and you keep straight on into Squires Lane. You are retracing the outward route. Turn left in front of Cavendish Lodge, pass the barn on your right and follow the track between hedges, then with fields on your left and the wood on your right. Take the first right turn onto the limestone track and follow it down through the woods to the campsite.

Rides 3 and 4

The following two rides are based at the village of Laxton where the medieval system of open field farming is still practised. A glance at the map of the parish shows that it has changed little over the centuries. Most of the farm houses and buildings are still right in the village centre, as they were in most parishes before enclosure. The surrounding agricultural land was usually divided into three fields, one for summer corn, one for winter corn, and one to lie fallow, plus common grazing land. The three main fields were then subdivided into many unfenced strips. Each farmer owned or rented many strips but the land was farmed virtually coopera-tively. When enclosure took place in other parishes, mostly in the 18th and 19th centuries, the land was divided more rationally. Each farmer acquired a plot of land which he then enclosed, and often also built a new farmhouse. A visit to the Laxton Visitor Centre will explain how the open field system worked in Laxton in the past and still does today. The first ride is on roads, the second is an off-road ride.

3. Laxton to Ossington

Distance: 9.5 miles
Route: Laxton – Ossington – Laxton
Surface: Tarmac.
Start: Laxton (SK725670)
Map: O.S. Landranger 120
Parking: The Visitor Centre, Laxton.
Accommodation: There is a small Camping and Caravanning Club Site at The Dovecote Inn, Tel. 01777 871586. There is also B&B available in the village – for details, contact Ollerton Tourist Information Centre: Tel. 01623 824545.
Comment: This is a pleasant ride on quiet country lanes with some hills.

The Journey

The ride begins at The Dovecote Inn, Laxton, where the Visitor Centre is housed in a range of out-buildings and the rear grassed area is a camp site. The Dovecote does serve meals, which smell delicious, but do not stay open all day. From the Inn car park turn left onto the road. On your right immediately is the site of one of the great houses of one of the village's major families, the Lexingtons. All that remains today are traces of fishponds. Three brothers of the family became famous in the 13th century, Robert, judge and soldier, John, Lord Keeper of the Great Seal, and Henry, Bishop of Lincoln. Continue down the road between handsome red brick farm houses and farm buildings to a fork in the road, take the right fork.

This road runs between Mill Field on your right and South Field on your left. After crossing a stream it climbs quite steeply between two woods to a crossroads, turn left here, signposted to Ossington. This is a quiet lane through farmland with South Field now on your left. Where the lane is unfenced it would appear there may have been an airfield perhaps during the last war. Then you are into the hamlet of Ossington, home of the Cartwrights and more recently the Denisons, in the 18th century. Ossington Hall was demolished in 1963 but hidden among the trees is a truly lovely church. To visit the church of the Holy Rood, continue straight on at the road junction and turn left down a lane just beyond a row of houses among trees. The lane bears right but you continue through the gates to Ossington Park, signposted 'Private', and along a track through the woods which turns left,

Laxton Parish Church

then right. Here the cool Classical lines of the church, built in 1782 on the site of a 12th century church, are complemented by beautiful trees and shrubs. Look for the unusual sun dial behind the church. The interior is worth a visit but the church is locked, details of where to collect the key on the church door.

There are footpaths through the Park but you must return to the road, turn right by the row of modern houses and right again at the junction in Ossington. Continue along this lane to Moorhouse where there is a short optional diversion to a chapel behind a farmyard, which may be clarty (as they say up north). To visit the chapel, turn down the lane on the right beside a red telephone box. The route continues, turning left just beyond the phone box, signposted to Laxton. Continue along this lane, with South Field on your left, to re-enter Laxton in the bottom of the village. Turn right and return to The Dovecote Inn.

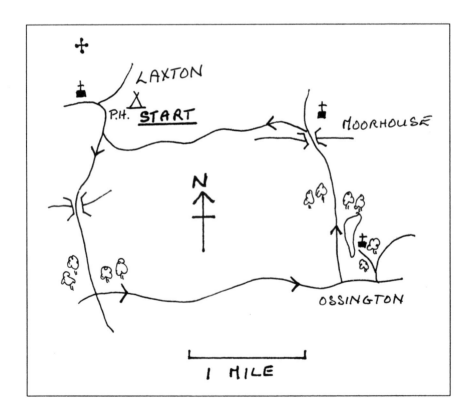

4. Laxton to Ompton

Distance: 10 miles

Route: Laxton – Ompton – Kneesall – Laxton

Surface: Rough dirt bridle path; tarmac; good farm tracks; green lanes.

Start: Laxton (SK725670)

Map: O.S. Landranger 120

Parking: Visitor Centre, Laxton.

Accommodation: Camping and Caravanning Club Site, Dovecote Inn, Laxton. Tel. 01777 871586. B&B available at Lilac Farm, Tel. 01777 870376. For more details contact Newark Tourist Information Centre, Tel. 01636 78962.

Comment: This is a real country ride using mostly farm tracks and returning to Laxton through Mill Field, one of Laxton's open fields. There is one short tough section of bridle-path close to the start and a few hills, but nothing too strenuous.

The Journey

From The Dovecote Inn car park run down to the road and, engaging a low gear, take the road opposite and slightly right which runs west and passes the church. Do not take the turning sharp right to Egmanton as you leave the car park. The church of St Michael, on your left has some funny gargoyles, including one with pointed ears climbing on the parapet. Inside there are several monuments to the two great families of the parish, the Lexingtons and the Everinghams. The last of the Everinghams, Baron Reginald Everingham, died in 1399 and an effigy of him and two other knights of the family lie in the church. One of the other two is of Robert de Everingham, died 1287, who was the last of the Chief Lords and Keepers of the Royal Forests. You can visit the site of the Norman castle that was home to the Everinghams, and lies to the north of the village, at the end of the ride.

Continue west along the lane through the village, there is a farm museum on your right, and out into open country with Mill Field on your left and West Field on your right. Westwood Farm stands on the left on a slight kink in the road, then there is a small copse on the right. Take the unfenced, signed bridle-path across the field on the left towards a wood. You are crossing Laxton Common, shown as Westwood Common on the old maps. This bridle-path was very rough after a wet winter. There is only a short stretch in the wood and then it gradually improves. At the junction of bridleways in the wood turn left and leave the trees for more open farmland.

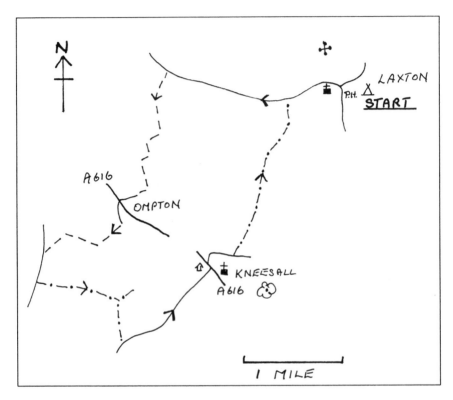

The bridle-path drops down a slope to a T-junction with a track. Turn right onto this increasingly good farm track and continue to another T-junction with the drive to Shortwood Farm which is on the higher land on your left. Turn right and follow the drive down until it reaches a small stream or ditch. Turn right, crossing over the stream and when the lane forks go left into Shortwood Farm Lane. You are now in the tiny hamlet of Ompton which, like Laxton, was also part of Geoffrey Alselin's estate in 1086.

Cross straight over the A616 into a 'No Through Road' with a phone box on the left corner. The lane becomes a track and at the T-junction turn right. This obviously ancient sunken road ends at a large dung heap. A bridle-path continues across a field beyond the dung heap, bearing slightly left and heading towards three strange grey pyramids which prove to be Water board buildings when you reach them. The bridle-path swings left before reaching them and continues out to a smartly mown grass verge. Turn left onto the road and take the second track on the left signposted to Leyfields Farm.

Keep straight on between the farm buildings and when you reach a junction turn right. The lane drops downhill to a road. Turn left onto the road and soon you will begin an increasingly stiff climb into Kneesall. As you come into the village, before the A616, there is Kingston Farm on the right and Old Hall Farmhouse on the left. This is a magnificent house, reputed to be the oldest brick house in the county, and stands on the site of a manor house mentioned in the Domesday Book.

Turn left onto the A616 and immediately right to cross the village green, then right again. Continue through the village into open country again and take the first track on the left, a wide compacted earth track. This is a good farm track and leads you across Laxton's open field called Mill Field, most of which is enclosed today. The track drops downhill to a stream, becoming grassy as it does so. After crossing the stream the grassy track climbs the hill

The church clock, Laxton – and we've missed the pub again!

beyond. There are a couple of tracks going off to the right, ignore these and continue to the hill top, on a clear day you can see Lincoln Cathedral. As you continue through Mill Field there is an information board on the right along the track explaining the open field system. This is part of an official walk around Laxton and you may meet other visitors around here.

When the track reaches the road turn right and freewheel downhill into Laxton. Stop at the church and take the green track opposite. There is an information board here too. The track leads to the site of the Norman Castle. There is nothing of the castle remaining, only the ditched mound where the timber tower stood. This is high ground for Nottinghamshire, with commanding views of what was then the Royal Forest of Sherwood. No wonder it was the home of Robert de Everingham, Chief Lord and Keeper of the Royal Forest. There is also a fine view of the village from here.

Return to the road, turn left and you are virtually at the Dovecote Inn where the ride began. Do visit the information Centre and buy a booklet on the village before dropping into the Inn for refreshments.

Rides 5 to 8

The following four rides are based in The Dukeries, an area of the King of England's medieval hunting ground in Sherwood Forest where land was given to several favoured Dukes on which to create Country Estates. Magnificent country houses, model farms, and carefully planned estate villages were created by the Dukes of Portland, Newcastle, Kingston, and Norfolk in the 18th century. Though the area is immaculately groomed, the forest remains much as it was in the days of Robin Hood. Clumber Park roads are closed to vehicles at night.

5. Clumber Park: short ride

Distance: 6.5 miles

Route: Hardwick – Crookford Farm – Hardwick

Surface: Multitudinous! Tarmac, good, soft (and occasionally treacherously sandy) forest paths, hard red shale bridle-paths, and good chalk farm tracks.

Start: Hardwick village (SK639754)

Map: O.S. Landranger 120 also the Nottinghamshire C.C. leaflet Ducal Nottinghamshire Eastern Circuit, Clumber to Crookford (produced primarily for equestrians).

Parking: Car park and toilets in Hardwick village.

Accommodation: Camping and Caravanning Club Site, The Walled Garden, Clumber Park. Tel. 01909 482303

Comment: This short ride, to the east of Clumber, passes through forest and farmland. It is a fairly gentle ride, with only one short stiff hill and two fords. Clumber Park has belonged to The National Trust since 1946, though the great house was demolished in 1938.

The Journey

The ride begins in Hardwick Village, only a short ride east from the Clumber Park camp site in the heart of the Park, and just west of the A614. To reach the village from the A614 turn off the main road, and enter the Park, opposite The Clumber Park Hotel (marked on the Ordnance Survey maps as Normanton Inn). Hardwick Village is a small Estate village, carefully laid out and beautifully built. The car park is just a gravel area beside impressive, farm buildings, which are unusual as they do not face south. The smart, modern toilets are in the rear of the left-hand building, and just beyond them is a large lake created by placing a weir across the River Poulter. Beside the lake, usually lined by fishermen, is an information board.

Leave the car park area with the cattleyards behind you and a farmyard on your right, turn right onto the lane through the village. This lane runs slightly downhill to the River Poulter where there is a ford and a footbridge. There is something ludicrously exciting about cycling through a ford, especially on a hot summer day – many cyclists 'collect' fords, like 'bagging' a Munro. Be warned, this one has an excellent stone base, with a slight slope to the east, which is covered with an almost invisible and slippery film of

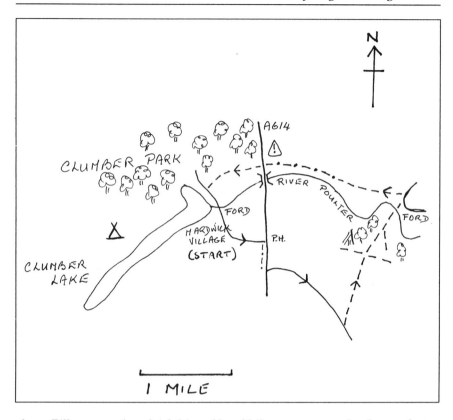

algae. Bill managed to dunk himself and bike on one crossing but unfortunately was on his feet too quickly for a photograph and refused to repeat the spectacle!

Stay on the tarmac lane, there is a bridle-path across a field on your left but the combination of hill and very sandy soil makes this unpleasant. The Robin Hood Way also follows this lane out to the A614. When you reach the A614 opposite the only hostelry on this ride, The Clumber Park Hotel, turn right onto a narrow path through the trees just outside the Park Gateway. This is a 'permissive path' parallel to the busy A614. Watch out for slippery tree roots and clutching branches from above as this path wends its way through the trees. Cross straight over West Drayton Avenue, another entrance to the Park, and continue through the trees to a small area with picnic tables. Turn left to the A614, go to the southern end of the layby and cross with care to the lane opposite signposted to Bothamsall.

This is a narrow and quiet country lane and it is quite a surprise to find nodding donkey engines pumping oil up from the depths. Beside them is a chalk farm track leading to a bridle-path across the field. Officially the bridle-path begins a little further on at the top of a slight rise but it appears unused and the farmer has not kept it clear. Bridle-path and chalk track meet almost under the power cables and the route continues along the main farm track over a small hill, passing unused buildings on your right and oil storage tanks on your left. At the bottom of the hill cross straight over the tarmac lane onto a dirt bridle-path through the crops. Watch out for soft sandy patches.

A water cannon was an unusual obstruction!

The path joins a good wide ride through the conifer wood. In an open area of heathland and silver birch, join a hard track which comes in from your right. There is a junction of several tracks here, keep straight ahead, do not take any tracks to the left. The track runs downhill to the River Poulter where there is another, very wide, ford. For those not wishing to get their feet wet again, there is a footbridge. Now the route joins a tarmac country lane on a huge bend. Keep straight on but do take care, the reason for the large bend is the container-truck base on the top of Crookford Hill to your right, when the lane narrows they fill the available space! However, you turn left, very soon, onto a bridleway, sign-posted 'West Bridge 1½.

After passing Crookford Farm the bridleway continues straight on through the trees ahead and then the fields with the River Poulter's reed beds on your left. Finally you reach the A614 along a short ridge of land with a narrow path edged with gorse, hawthorn, and brambles! Cross the A614, with care, and continue opposite along another bridle-path onto National Trust land. The path bends slightly left and runs beside a fence through the trees, keep left along the edge of an open field and turn left onto a tarmac lane.

This is one of the entrances to Hardwick's P.Y.O. Fruit Farm and Shop (selling picked fruit and vegetables, ices and local cider), so watch out for traffic. The route continues straight ahead through a gate marked clearly with blue arrows, between two hedges. When this track also turns right into the fruit farm keep straight on through another gate and downhill between fruit trees and rows of vegetables, take care you do not run down any pickers! Continue uphill and turn left when you reach tarmac in Hardwick village, watch-out for sleeping policemen, then turn right for the car park. Now you can go and sit by the lake to eat your strawberries.

6. Clumber Park. Corunna Lodge – a Sherwood Forest ride

Distance:	13 miles
Route:	Hardwick Village – Carburton – Corunna Lodge – Hardwick
Surface:	Wide variety from tarmac to soft pine needles.
Start:	As for the previous ride, Hardwick Village (SK639754)
Map:	O.S. Landranger 120 and Nottinghamshire County Council's 'Ducal Nottinghamshire Eastern Circuit, Clumber to Crookford'. For further exploration O.S. Pathfinder SK 47/57 & SK 67/77 would be useful.
Parking:	Hardwick Village, Clumber Park.
Accommodation:	Camping as previous ride, Clumber Park, Tel. 01909 482303.
Comment:	The previous ride only gave a minute taste of forest riding. This one is almost all in the forest with so many lovely diversions and picnic spots you will probably decide to stay for several days if you are camping and it may be worthwhile investing in the Pathfinder maps which cover this area. The ride does not include any serious hills but the countryside is not flat and it may be sensible to push up some rough or sandy slopes. It could be quite easy to get lost in such a heavily forested area, despite the good signposting, we would suggest you carry a compass, and learn how to use it!

The Journey

As with the previous ride Hardwick Village car park is the start. Leave the car park with the cattleyards behind you and the farmyard on your right. Turn left onto the lane through the village. You should be heading north west and uphill, with the treat of the ford for the return! Pass the bridle-path entrance to the PYO Fruit Farm on your right, the village War Memorial, then a vehicle entrance to the PYO Farm. Continue straight ahead but watch for a narrow signed bridleway among the trees on the left. This track is hard packed sandy soil, but watch for soft patches, and runs gently downhill. Cross straight over a tarmac lane onto a soft woodland track under conifers.

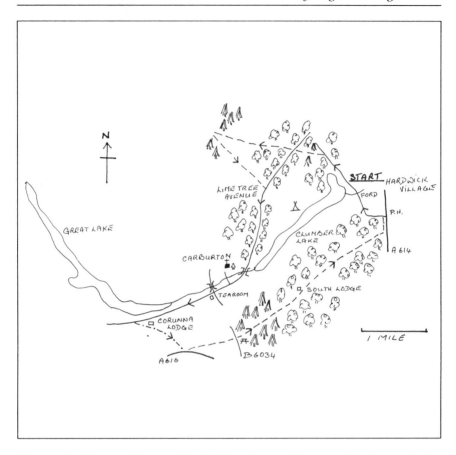

The smell of the conifers and the feeling that you have suddenly acquired a fully sprung bike is delightful.

When the track leaves the conifers turn right onto a wide track along the edge of the trees with, at first more open heathland on your left. Follow this track to the tarmac road. This is Lime Tree Avenue, once part of the drive to Clumber House. This magnificent, three mile, double avenue of Lime trees was planted in the 19th century by the 5th Duke of Newcastle and is reputed to contain 1296 trees. This time the route crosses straight over the avenue to a picnic area opposite. Pass to the right of the picnic area and leave it along a good stony track, half blocked by a large tree trunk. This path is red shale at first then limestone. Cross straight over a tarmac track into a less-wooded heathland area, then into the trees again.

Turn left by the telegraph pole by Forest Plantation Cottages and continue to the tarmac road. Cross straight over onto a long forest path. On reaching another road turn left then at crossroads turn right onto Lime Tree Avenue, here there are finger posts pointing to various interesting places in the Park. If it is a windy day this is probably the first time you will notice it, the forest trees seem to give plenty of shelter everywhere else but the wind is funnelled along the avenue, which is also hilly. The avenue swoops down and up before dropping down again to the River Poulter. The road crosses the river on a narrow bridge and leaves the Park through an even narrower gateway; listen out for approaching traffic.

Beyond Clumber Park the road follows closely beside the river and on the hill on the far side the tiny Norman church of St Giles, Carburton, stands among a few cottages and farmhouses. This unusual, rendered, building is all that remains of a much larger church and is well worth a short diversion if only to see the double sundial on the corner of the building near the door, and the views to the east, of Clumber Park, and to the west, of Welbeck Estate. The large farmhouse behind the church was built for John Mazine, equerry to the 1st Duke of Newcastle at the Battle of Marston Moor.

Continuing along the road the route crosses straight over the B6034 and passes to the right of the School House Tea Rooms then continues between the forest and the river. Soon you pass a small dam on the right and the river widens to form The Great Lake on the Welbeck Estate, the first of several lakes which stretch for three miles and were created in the 18th century. Every spare bit of roadside land is used for car parking by the anglers who congregate here, watch for opening car doors. You will also probably see a few photographers, with some interesting equipment, waiting patiently for the picture of a lifetime! The lakes play host to many waterfowl at different times of the year, including the lovely Great Crested Grebe, and the surrounding woods also house the largest heronry in Nottinghamshire.

The route passes Gibraltar Lodge, one of many almost identical stone lodges on the Welbeck Estate many of which were built with their kitchens underground. At Corunna Lodge, again on your left, which does not have a name plate but does have a small paddock and some kennels beside it, the route turns left onto a dirt track which passes behind the lodge. Do not be put off by the sign saying 'Private Woodland', the track is an unclassified country road. This is the first off-road section on the Welbeck Estate and the difference is immediately apparent. Clumber Park is maintained for the public with off-road paths in good condition, but Welbeck is a very private estate; the tracks and paths are less well-maintained, and you must not stray from the public right of way.

The track continues between fields and woodland, up and downhill, occasionally rough and steep enough to encourage walking, until you reach an open space used as a car park beside the A616. Many tracks leave this area – take the second on the left, signposted for the Robin Hood Way, which at first has the main road immediately on its right. This is a pleasant path which passes behind some kennels on your right and with woodland on the left. Watch out for a large white arrow painted on the ground and pointing to the right. Although the path appears to continue straight on the bridle-path turns right, then immediately left to continue parallel to line of the original path. There is a signpost but it is concealed by giant stinging nettles. There is an old hedge on your left and a field fence on the right; the path is narrow and deeply cut into the ground.

Cross straight over the B6034 to a picnic area. Continue straight ahead with the main picnic area to your right and through a gate into the forest. Immediately you are faced with a dilemma, two tracks. The Ordnance Survey map implies the left fork is the bridle-path, but a large sign forbids entry. Keep to the right-hand path and you will very soon be reassured by either a large white arrow or a Robin Hood Way sign. You now have Welbeck Estate on your left and Thoresby Estate, the home of the Dukes of Kingston upon Hull, on your right. The path you are cycling on is called Freeboard Lane, and was originally an area of "no man's land" between the two estates.

Keep left at the first fork, signposted as a bridleway; the phantom white arrow painter has been busy here too and the signs are a great help. Soon you reach South Lodge, a completely different style of building from the Welbeck lodges. This one is single storey with an interesting chimney; beside it are some handsome gates with a pair of patient greyhounds atop the gateposts. Keep straight ahead and continue to a picnic area just before the A614. There is no vehicular access to this area, just a layby on the main road and a few picnic tables in a clearing.

Turn left, before reaching the road, on a narrow path through the shrubbery and towards a fallen tree. Once clear of the shrubs the path is obvious. This is a 'permissive path' which enables walkers, cyclists and equestrians to avoid using the narrow A614. The path spills out of the forest onto a tarmac entrance to Clumber Park, Drayton Avenue; cross straight over into the trees again. This path has more low branches and sneaky tree roots to avoid! When you reach the next tarmac lane you will see The Clumber Park

Hotel on the far side of the A614. Turn left on the lane and enter Clumber Park through the gateway. Follow the tarmac lane when it bends right and continue to the ford across the River Poulter. You will see from the previous ride that this can be dangerously slippery for cyclists and we recommend using the footbridge. Ahead of you is Hardwick Village, you are back at the start of the ride.

The handsome 'Greyhound' gates at the South Lodge entrance to Clumber Park

7. Creswell Crags

Distance:	6 miles
Route:	Welbeck – Creswell – Holbeck – Norton – Welbeck
Surface:	Tarmac, grass.
Start:	Lady Margaret Hall, Welbeck Estate SK551734
Map:	O.S. Landranger 120 & Nottinghamshire County Council's Ducal Nottinghamshire Western Circuit, Creswell to Carburton.
Parking:	Difficult if not camping! Possible to start the ride at Creswell Crags and use their car park.
Accommodation:	Lady Margaret Hall Camping and Caravanning Club site, Welbeck Estate. Simple site with drinking water, toilet, and hand basin.
Comment:	This is the first of two rides based at Lady Margaret Hall campsite. It is a short one which will give you time to visit both Creswell Crags and the Dukeries Adventure Park. There is a stiff climb out of Creswell, the first part on tarmac, the second on a dirt bridleway used by tractors. Two short sections of main road are used, the A616 has a footpath.

The Journey

The campsite is a large field just off the A60, behind a lodge house, and opposite a turning to Holbeck. The Park road used to reach it is a private road; there is footpath access to the village of Norton but no cycle access. Leave the campsite and cross the A60, with care, into the lane signposted to Holbeck. Almost immediately you are in a small cluster of houses which is Holbeck Woodhouse. On the left is a village shop and opposite is a lane that will take you to the church and on to the far side of Holbeck. As this is a footpath, continue along the road through the village. Shortly the road makes a sharp left bend but you keep straight on up the steep hill ahead signposted 'Danger Concealed Entrance'. This lane is extremely narrow and deeply cut through red sandstone.

At the top of the hill bear right at the road junction, then right again at the T-junction. You are now in the village of Holbeck with a magnificent view of the surrounding countryside. When the road swings sharp left there is a covered gateway on your right which not only leads to a footpath to the church but also frames a view of Welbeck Abbey. Continue along the road

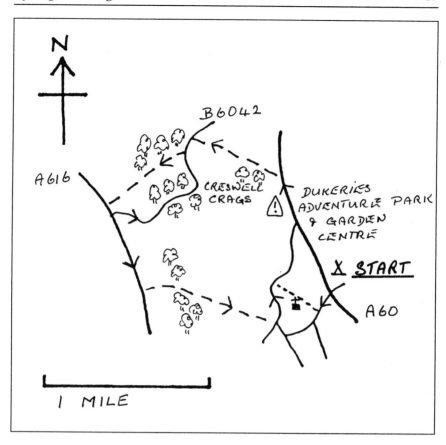

which quickly drops downhill again, passing on the way the church drive (footpath) from Holbeck Woodhouse.

Turn left onto the A60. This road is narrow and there is no pavement but you leave it in about a quarter of a mile. First there is the Dukeries Adventure Park and Garden Centre on the right; these are worth at least a short visit if only to see some of the Welbeck Abbey estate such as the walled garden, a glass-covered arcade for exercising horses in bad weather, and the estate's gas works. Continue along the A60 to a lodge house on the left. Turn left beside it onto a bridle-path along an estate drive.

When this drive reaches a five-bar gate, turn right onto a farm track. (It is possible to detour to Creswell Crags from the gate but this is a footpath only.) Follow the farm track to the far side of the field then turn left in front of the gate, onto a field path. Leave this field through a narrow gap in the hedge onto a narrow road. The vision is poor here, so take care and listen for approaching traffic. Turn left onto this road and immediately right onto another signed bridleway, this time a wide path with hedges either side and glimpses of a large quarry through the trees on the right. There is a short climb then a long gentle run down to Creswell with some magnificent farm buildings close to the bottom.

Turn left onto the A616 and almost immediately left again for Creswell Crags Visitor Centre. The route has been in Derbyshire since leaving the A60 but the two counties meet along the line of the Crags. There are toilets and refreshments available at the centre, and car parking. This is the alternative start to the ride for those who are not camping. The caves of Creswell Crags have yielded some very interesting finds including the bones of reindeer, bison, bear, hippopotamus, wolf, rhinoceros and humans, giving clues to life in this part of the world 70,000 years ago.

When you have seen enough return to the A616 and turn left. This road is quite busy and fast but there is no real problem until you start to climb the hill. Luckily there is a footpath here. Well up the hill is a signed bridle-path on the left. Turn onto this path which is bordered by a tangle of brambles and hawthorn. It is fairly rough and obviously used by farm vehicles, and it may be easier to walk as it climbs the side of the valley to a belt of trees. Beyond the trees there is open farmland but the track is sheltered by hedges. When it divides close to Holbeck, take the right track and continue to the road.

Cross straight over the road into a narrow lane (one you used at the start of the ride). Take the left fork and drop down the steep hill into Holbeck Woodhouse and retrace the start of the route to the campsite.

8. Welbeck Abbey

Distance:	13 miles
Route:	Welbeck – Norton – Carburton – Clumber Park – Welbeck
Surface:	Tarmac, grass, and forest rides (sometimes sandy, often thick pine needles).
Start:	Lady Margaret Hall Camping & Caravanning Club site, Welbeck Estate. (SK551734)
Map:	O.S. Landranger 120 & Nottinghamshire County Council's Ducal Nottinghamshire Western Circuit, Creswell to Carburton.
Parking:	Difficult unless you park at the National Trust car park in Clumber Park and join the ride on Lime Tree Avenue.
Accommodation:	Lady Margaret Hall Camping & Caravanning site, Welbeck Abbey Estate, on the A60, near Holbeck Woodhouse. A simple green site with basic toilet and washing facilities.
Comment:	This ride links with, and covers some of the same ground as, the Eastern Clumber Park ride. It is probably 50% tarmac and 50% forest rides. There are no serious hills. Do not use the Welbeck Estate roads, other than the official Rights of Way, they are strictly private.

The Journey

From the campsite, cross the A60 into the lane, signposted to Holbeck. Pass the Holbeck Woodhouse village shop on your left and follow the road through the village as it bends sharp left. This lane is narrow but you can see traffic coming as the land ahead rises, watch over the hedge-tops. At the off-set crossroads turn left and continue to the A60. Watch to your right and you will catch a glimpse of the tower of the Norman church of Cuckney, St Mary's. During restoration of this church in 1950 a mass grave was discovered under the nave containing 50 skeletons believed to be those of soldiers killed in the Civil Wars of 1135 to 1154. Cuckney also has a hostelry which may be worth a visit later in the day if you are camping at Lady Margaret Hall.

The route crosses straight over the A60 into Norton lane. Again this is narrow and used by double-decker buses, so keep your ears open for approaching traffic. When you reach the village of Norton turn left at the

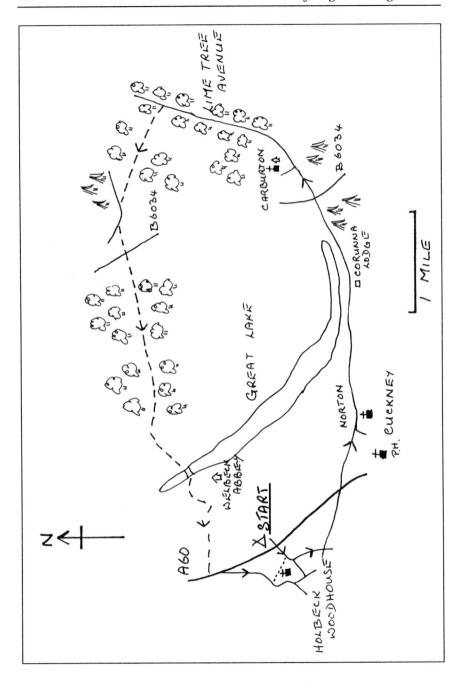

T-junction, signposted to Clumber, and follow the road round to the right by the Best Kept Village sign. There is a footpath from the campsite to Norton through the Welbeck Estate (not open to cyclists) which would make a pleasant evening walk. Continue along the road which makes a sharp right bend at another entrance to Welbeck Estate. If you are going fishing this gateway gives access to the Lakes on your left. However, many fishermen prefer to park beside the road, and from this point the not very wide road is lined with an assortment of fishermen's and photographers vehicles. Engrossed in gathering all their equipment together they may not check before opening their doors, so take care.

Just after passing Bentinck Lodge on your right, you pass a handsome monument to Lord George Bentinck, the third son of the fourth Duke of Portland, who died near here in 1848 aged 47, while walking from Welbeck to Thoresby. The monument is a public water fountain for both man and beast: note the low dog bowl to the left. Lord Bentinck was thought to be a potential Prime Minister and if Disraeli's tribute is half true he would have been an asset to the country. It is worth pausing here just to read it and to note the wide sweep of green road approaching the monument from the south.

To the left of the road are Welbeck's lakes and dams and a wealth of waterbirds. Corunna Lodge, un-named, is next on your right. This is where the Clumber Park ride takes the dirt track behind the lodge. On this ride you stay on the road. Note the design of the lodges, they are all identical and very substantial buildings. Apparently they were built with the kitchen and toilets underground and it was common to see smoke issuing from the ground. This subterranean foible of the 5th Duke of Portland was highly developed and you see further evidence later in the ride.

The road continues beside the River Poulter with a steep bank of pines on the right, and reaches an off-set crossroads with the B6034. On your right is the School House Tea Rooms where good home cooking should be available. Cross straight over, signposted to Clumber and Carburton. The church of St Giles, Carburton, stands on rising ground on the left and is worth a brief diversion. In early '94 the plastered walls looked grey and uninviting but workmen were busy laying new floors and spraying the timbers against death-watch beetle and woodworm. Perhaps the exterior may receive some attention too. The church is Norman and the light interior contains a memorial to John Mazine (for whom Manor Farm behind the church was built) who was equerry to the 1st Duke of Newcastle at the Battle of Marston Moor. On the outside of the church is an unusual double sun dial.

After visiting the church return to the route which continues past Carburton and enters Clumber Park through a narrow gateway flanked by gate houses. Visibility here is poor, so listen for both approaching traffic and also horses which may be startled by the sudden appearance of cyclists. The road crosses the River Poulter and enters Lime Tree Avenue. This magnificent three-mile double avenue (the black bands around the trunks are a form of pest control) was created in the 18th century by the 5th Duke of Newcastle. The grass avenues on either side of the road are not part of the public highway and you are requested not to ride on them.

The avenue is an undulating road with some beautiful picnicking spots and magnificent beeches beyond the limes on either side of the road. Clumber Park is now owned by the National Trust and there are several turnings to the right, clearly signposted, which will take you on a diversion

The Robin Hood Way in the Manor Hills Forest

to the National Trust facilities which include a shop, restaurant, toilets, campsite, etc. After one of these junctions the lime tree avenue is interrupted by an area of heathland. On the far side of this open area the lime tree avenue begins again and there is another crossroads. Here the route turns left on the tarmac lane signposted to Trumans Lodge, then immediately take the red shale, signposted, bridleway on the right. Very soon you will notice Robin Hood Way signs which confirm that you are on the correct track.

Apart from a short stretch of tarmac bridleway used by vehicles the route now continues on quiet bridleways almost back to the campsite. This first one is a hard packed trail first through broadleaved woodland then through tall conifers. On reaching a tarmac lane turn left onto this which is actually a bridleway though it is shown as a yellow minor road on the O.S. maps. Whatever it is this strip of tarmac links the A57 with the B6034 along the northern edge of the National Trust land, so take care. At Trumans Lodge, an entrance to Clumber Park, bear right with the tarmac and in a short distance enter the wood on the left beside a five-bar gate. There is a bridleway signpost here.

The trees with the large shiny leaves are sweet chestnut and in a good season the ground will be thick with the shells of the nuts. This tree was introduced to Britain by the Romans who made flour from the nuts but though the tree does well on Nottinghamshire's light sandy soil the nuts rarely mature in this country.

The path continues to the B6034, the Ollerton Road. Cross with care and keep straight ahead on a continuation of the bridle-path known as Drinking Pit Lane. Deep in the wood you come to Old Toll Bar Lodge which stands at an old disused crossroads of tracks. Pass this squat stone building, keeping it on your left and follow the path that crosses a tarmac drive and ornamental gates, beside Lady Bolsover Drive Lodge. The Nottinghamshire County Council leaflet tells you to take the left fork when the path divides shortly but the right path is fairly insignificant and you may well miss it; just keep on the main path which soon drops down a narrow cleft between miniature red sandstone cliffs.

At the bottom of quite a steep run down the path bends to the right and can be a trifle wet, take care. The path follows the metal fence to South Lodge. The route turns left before the lodge but first look at the front of the lodge, which is an entrance to Welbeck Abbey. The lodges look unusual and the gate is extremely unusual as it is made of wood and painted black. Normally these fancy entrances have delicate wrought iron gates as the Lady Bolsover Drive has. Return to the route, entering the estate through the deer park gates and following signs for Welbeck Abbey, then right through a bridle-gate and up a bank.

Here the oddity is revealed, or rather not revealed. The lodge gates are built into a small hillside and there appears to be no entrance to the estate behind them. But there is! Remember those underground kitchens? This is an underground entrance to Welbeck Abbey! From here a tunnel, a mile and a quarter long and large enough for a horse and carriage, runs underground across the fields and under the lake. Your path goes through another bridlegate then follows beside the line of the tunnel across the fields to the lake. A wild tangle of grassy vegetation grows along the top of the tunnel and the depressions indicate where the skylights were placed at 12 yard intervals. The tunnel is now unsafe, do not be tempted to walk on it.

Cycling across the field keep your eyes on the trees ahead and slightly left. This is where you will catch the only glimpse of Welbeck Abbey. The Abbey was founded in 1153 for the Order of Premonstratensian Canons by Thomas de Cuckney. After the dissolution Henry VIII gave it to Richard Whalley. Over the years families have varying fortunes and the Whalleys eventually sold the Abbey to Bess of Hardwick. This industrious lady, a penniless bride at 14, became a wealthy widow a year later, and from the age of thirty she married and outlived two more wealthy husbands before marrying the Earl of Shrewsbury. Bess began the building of the great house at Welbeck for her son and a few generations later the estate passed, by marriage, into the hands of the Dukes of Portland.

The 5th Duke of Portland was obviously an eccentric, he went far beyond building the odd folly. Apart from the tunnel, he built a whole suite of rooms under the great house which included a ballroom, 174ft long and 22ft high, and three libraries 250ft long – though what a man reputed to have a morbid fear of being seen needed with a ballroom, above or below ground, is a puzzle. At the time of his death in 1879 he had 15,000 men employed on 36 different subterranean projects around the estate. He may have been mad, but what an employer!

The route crosses a flat bridge of land between two lakes as it enters the grounds of the house, then swings sharp right. Shortly a path swings off through the trees on the left – do not take it. Take the bridle-path on the left a little further on, which climbs a slight rise with a small wood on the left and an open field on the right. The path narrows with a fence on the left and the school playing fields beyond. Continue to a concrete track and turn right. There is a cattle grid, with a way past it to the right. This track climbs a rise between open fields then descends to a crossroads of tracks. Go straight across, passing a lodge on your left and at the next junction take the left fork which is an ornamental drive with small conifers on either side.

This drive will take you out to the A60. Turn left onto this road and take great care. On the left shortly is the entrance to The Dukeries Adventure Park and Garden Centre. If you wish to see more of Welbeck Abbey buildings, take a diversion: the Garden Centre is in the walled garden and the glass houses of 1874 are being restored. Close by are the 5th Duke's glass covered horse gallops and the gas works installed to light his subterranean world.

The route continues on the A60 past the entrance to the Dukeries Adventure Park and takes the first lane on the right, signposted to Holbeck. Take the second lane on the left which is gated and a footpath only. This is only a short walk which takes you along a lime avenue past St Winifred's church, built in 1913 in the Norman style, to another gate. Turn left and follow the lane to the A60. Cross straight over to the campsite.

9. Southwell to Farnsfield

Distance:　　　　11 miles circular from Southwell. 16 miles if starting from Brinkley.

Route:　　　　　Brinkley – Southwell – Halam – Farnsfield – Southwell – Brinkley.

Surface:　　　　Tarmac and tracks which vary from excellent to muddy when wet, and a firm cinder trail.

Start:　　　　　Brinkley campsite (SK721526). Alternatively Southwell Trail Car Park (SK706545), which would reduce the overall mileage by five miles.

Map:　　　　　O.S. Landranger 120

Accommodation: The Orchards campsite, Brinkley, Southwell, Nottinghamshire, NG25 0TP. Tel. 01623 635725. This is a 'no frills' site with chemical loos and no shower. It is a pleasant quiet spot with views across the Trent Valley, and a shop selling, among other things, home produced vegetables.

There is a variety of other accommodation available in Southwell, contact Nottinghamshire County Council, Tel. 0115 977 4212 for details.

Comment:　　　The first half of this ride is hilly but the hard work is rewarded with some magnificent views and several great downhills. Part of the return is along Southwell Trail (a disused Railway Track) which is flat and sheltered but possibly busy at weekends. The ride uses minor roads and tracks and a few stretches can be dodgy after rain.

This is the first of two rides based at Brinkley. This first one is definitely a gardeners' ride with nurseries and garden centres too numerous to mention. Many private gardens are a picture and some are open to the public a few days a year. See The National Gardens Scheme leaflet for details, available from Nottinghamshire County Council, telephone number above.

The Journey

Turn right out of The Orchards campsite. The hills begin immediately with a climb, but there are Nurseries and Garden Centres every hundred yards or so to distract you from your efforts. Southwell Garden Centre also has a tea shop! The road then drops down to Easthorpe, where the Bramley Apple

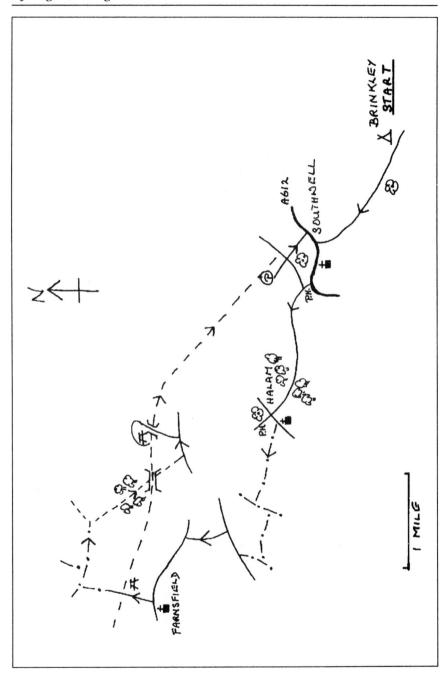

was first grown from an apple seed by a Mrs Brailsford in 1805. A Mr Merryweather realised the fruit's potential and you pass the Merryweather Garden Centre and Bramley Apple Exhibition after leaving Southwell.

Turn left onto the A612 for Southwell.

This is an historic town, famous for its roses and the Minster dating from 1110 AD. The Minster, on your left as you approach the town centre, is refreshingly simple and reassuringly solid. There are many interesting features to distract you from your ride, from the original Norman building to the 19th century 'pepperpots' which crown the towers, and inside some beautiful carving from the late 19th century. Beyond the Minster are the ruins of the Bishops Palace where Cardinal Wolsey lived for a time after his fall from favour. There are many splendid houses in Southwell, mostly red brick and pantiles, with walls leaning drunkenly at odd angles and some fine old windows.

When the A612 turns left at a mini roundabout in front of the Saracen's Head, where Charles I spent his last night as a free man in 1645, you turn right and immediately left into Queens Street. On your right is a large baker's shop with displays of wickedly tempting cakes and a wide range of wholesome breads.

Leaving Southwell behind the route passes the Merryweather Garden Centre, with Bramley Apple Exhibition and Tea Room, before beginning to climb again. Up Norwood Hill with fruit orchards on either side of the road, a splendid sight at blossom time, and then down Halam Hill to the village of Halam. Turn left at the crossroads into Radley Road. On the left is another 12th century church with a short solid tower, an entrance low enough to make almost everyone duck, and a comforting and well-loved interior lit by beautiful windows which include panels by William Morris and Byrne-Jones. After leaving the church turn right into Gray Lane.

Keep straight on until, after passing yet another Nursery on your right, the lane becomes a dirt track. This track can be the most difficult section of the ride, not least because it climbs from less than 50 metres to about 80 metres, but mainly as it can be muddy. In early spring after a very wet winter we have been forced to walk most of this half mile. At the top of the hill, with the entrance to New Hall Farm opposite, turn left onto a narrow tarmac lane and climb the hill to a Reservoir. Turn right onto another dirt track, not so muddy or difficult this time as it runs around the contours of the hill. After passing a farm on your left the track joins a tarmac lane, turn right. This is a steep drop down with banks of wild violets bordering the narrow lane in spring. On reaching a cluster of houses and a T-junction turn right again.

Take the first turning on the left and left again at the T-junction onto the road from Southwell to Farnsfield which you left in Halam.

Farnsfield was the birthplace of the explorer Augustus Charles Gregory who mapped much of the Australian Outback in 1855. Just before reaching the church, there is a lane on the right called New Hill that is the continuation of your route. First, visit the churchyard of the red brick church and see if you can find the tombstone of the 1740 blacksmith, William Butler.

Those interested in butterflies and farm animals could make a diversion from the route here by continuing along the road past the church for a little over a mile to the Butterflies Pleasure Park, and The White Post Modern Farm Centre.

The flanks of a Nottinghamshire hillside, and not a coal mine in sight!

Continuing, New Hill soon becomes Broomfield Lane (a habit of British roads that infuriates and confounds our American cousins!). Just after passing the last house it crosses the route of an old railway which is now The Robin Hood Way and The Southwell Trail. For a quick return to Southwell, shortening the route by a mile and a half, join the Trail on your right. Continue along the lane as it passes between a pair of round gate posts. At the T-junction turn right. Upper Hargreave and Hargreave Park, where the remains of a Roman Villa have been found, are along the next lane on the left, but you keep straight on to Timberlea Stud Farm with inquisitive foals and yearlings gambolling cheekily in the fields on the right. Keep straight on with the stable block on your left and a large stone house on your right.

Through the gate ahead are two tracks that bear left and right. Take the right track across open fields. This begins as a firm farm track but after it forks, you take the left fork, which becomes more of a dirt track. The track continues between an avenue of horse chestnut trees to Spring Farm. Continue past the farm, passing under the Southwell Trail, and out to the road. Turn left and take first left sign-posted Kirklington. Pass a smallholding on your left, cross a railway bridge and immediately turn left to a picnic site on the Southwell Trail. On reaching the Trail the picnic site is to the right and your route to the left.

From here The Southwell Trail is a two and a half mile, well-maintained, cinder track which wends a sheltered way to a car park close to the River Greet on the south east edge of Southwell. From the car park turn right onto the road and left at the crossroads into Burgage. It was here that in 1804 Lord Byron's mother rented Burgage Manor, on the edge of Burgage Green, where Byron spent his holidays during his time at Cambridge University.

Those returning to The Orchard campsite continue to the junction with the A612, turn right, signposted to Lowdham, then turn left into Fiskerton Road. The road climbs then swoops down to the camp site.

10. Southwell to Thurgarton

Distance: 15 miles

Route: Brinkley – Southwell – Westhorpe – Thurgarton – Bleasby – Morton – Brinkley.

Surface: Minor roads; farm tracks; one short section muddy after rain.

Start: The Orchards Camping & Caravanning Site (SK721526)

Map: O.S. Landranger 120 & 129 & Nottinghamshire County Council's leaflet for equestrians 'Epperstone Park to Southwell Minster.

Accommodation: The Orchards Camping & Caravanning Site, Tel. 01623 635725, is an inexpensive and simple site just outside Southwell. For other accommodation and further details of the area contact: Newark Tourist Information Tel. 01636 78962.

Comment: A climb to start the ride, but then a long gentle drop down to the Trent Valley. The ride includes a short section of rough track around fields, which is not too far to walk, but mostly uses good farm tracks highly suitable for mixed ability riders. This ride links with Nottinghamshire County Council's Epperstone Park to Southwell Minster route for mountain bikers and horse riders, watch out for their blue arrows. Their route includes more off-road work, some of which can be very difficult after rain.

If you are interested in gardens, check with the National Gardens Scheme leaflet as private gardens are sometimes open to the public (Thurgarton; Bleasby; Fiskerton; Brinkley; Southwell) on or close to the route throughout the year. Leaflet available from most Tourist Offices and Libraries.

The Journey

Turn right towards Southwell out of the camp site and instantly begin to climb passing several Nurseries and Garden Centres. Opposite a terrace of red brick cottages turn left along Crink Lane which passes round the hill above Southwell giving excellent views of the Minster. Turn right at the T-junction and keep right at the next junction that will take you down to the main road with the rugby ground on your right. Turn right onto the A612,

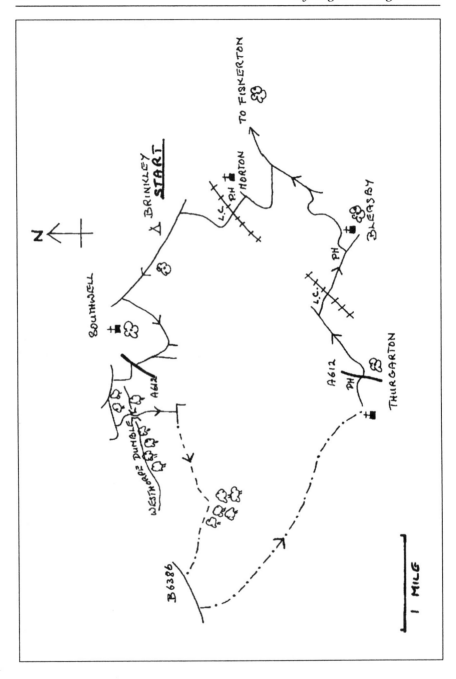

taking great care, then immediately left into Halloughton Road. This road makes a sharp right bend crosses a stream and climbs to the B6386 in Southwell. Turn left onto the B6386 at the T-junction. The houses and gardens of Southwell are so attractive take care you do not miss the next turning in less than a quarter of a mile!

Where several roads join the B6386, take the left fork ahead with a row of cottages called Sunnyside on your right. Take the lane to the left with the sign The Holme on the end of the cottage on the corner. The lane climbs then drops down Cundy Hill to Westhorpe Dumble, a narrow stream in a densely wooded valley. The climb out of the valley is steep, giving plenty of time to contemplate the age of the deeply sunken lane. At the top of the hill, when the lane makes a sharp left bend, turn right towards Stubbins Farm. There

A good path through a young plantation

is a bridle-path sign here. When the farm track turns sharp right keep straight on as the track begins to cross several fields. This is the part that can be very muddy in wet conditions. Keep the hedge on your right until after passing under the electricity cables the track goes through a hedge ahead. Turn left and go round the edge of the field to a gateway into Halloughton Wood.

The path ahead is a well-maintained cinder path leading through Cotmoor Plantation and out to the B6386. Turn left onto this road and in about half a mile turn left again along a lane to Thurgarton Quarters Farm. This is an old lane, with great views across the surrounding farm land and across Halloughton Dumble to Halloughton Wood to the east and towards Thistly Coppice and the site of a Roman Villa to the west. The lane passes straight through the farmyard and just beyond the next farm, Bankwood Farm, begins to descend towards Thurgarton. The last farm on the track is Hill Farm, owned by the Boots Company who also own Thurgarton Priory beside the handsome church.

As you come down the hill the squat tower of the church appears through the trees with a magnificent 13th century doorway reputed to be the best in England. St Peters church is all that remains of an Augustinian Priory founded by Ralph d'Eyncourt. Inside the church, to the left of the entrance, is a plan showing the extent of the original buildings which then boasted twin towers similar to Southwell Minster.

The lane continues down past the church into the lovely village of Thurgarton with its beautiful gardens, some open to the public a few days in the year, and a small stream gurgling beside the road. On reaching the A612 cross almost straight over into Bleasby Road. Follow the road through Goverton and into Bleasby, passing the inviting Manor Farm Tea shop with its 1736 dovecote on your left, and turn left along Gipsy Lane just before reaching the church. On the left here is The Wagon and Horses, for those who prefer something stronger than tea!

This is a narrow twisting lane, so take care and listen for approaching traffic. At the next junction turn left and take the first turning on the left. This will take you into Morton where you turn left again just before The Full Moon, though you may be tempted to stop again, perhaps for a meal this time. The lane rattles over a level crossing, bends sharp right, and at the T-junction turn left again and almost immediately the caravans at the Orchard Caravan Site are visible across the hedges on your right.

11. Eakring

Distance:	10.5 miles
Route:	Farnsfield – Bilsthorpe – Eakring – Kirklington – Farnsfield
Surface:	Tarmac & firm Trail (optional off-road a mixture of good track and decidedly dicey, dirt path)
Start:	Southwell Trail Picnic Site, Farnsfield. (SK644572)
Parking:	Southwell Trail Picnic Site
Map:	O.S. Landranger 120
Accommodation:	Camping – Possibly opening in 1995 Butterflies, White Post, Farnsfield. Tel. 01623 882773
	Farmhouse Accommodation – Dower House, Lower Hexgreave Fm., Farnsfield, Newark, Notts. NG22 8BJ, Tel. 01623 882020
Comment:	This ride begins and ends on Trails along disused railways where gradients are gentle. However, there are steep gradients on the road sections, both up and down. The off-road option is not suitable after wet weather, or for the inexperienced. It includes a narrow muddy path which is crossed by many tree roots requiring expert riding. This section also includes a short footpath linking a bridle-path to farm tracks.

The Journey

The ride starts from the Farnsfield picnic site on the Southwell Trail. To reach this from the centre of Farnsfield, take New Hill, almost opposite the church, then the second left into Station Lane and watch for the 'Picnic Site 200 yds' sign. Turn right here and follow the track to the car park. In the car park a sign points southeast along the old track to both Bilsthorpe and Southwell. Set off in this direction but take the first path to the left among a jungle of broom. This will take you to the start of the trail to Bilsthorpe which runs almost due north. The track is firm and well-maintained, and irons out the humps in the terrain nicely, also passing safely under the A617.

Turning unwanted railway tracks into safe, off-road paths for walkers, cyclists, and horse riders seems so sensible that the charity Sustrans, who have pioneered this work all over the country should receive as much encouragement as possible. There are two drawbacks to these routes: first,

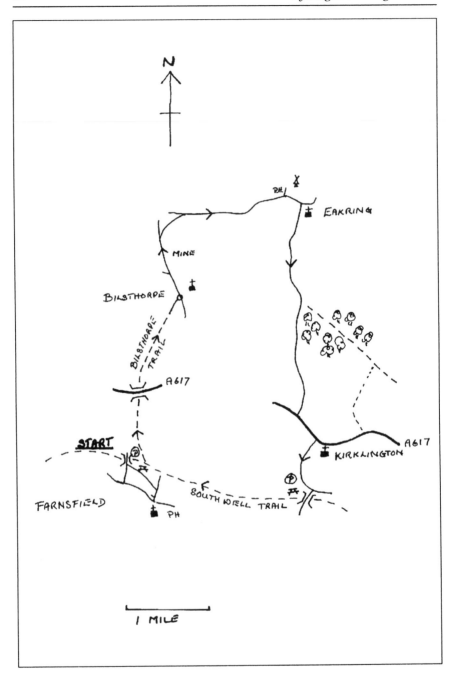

N

PH.

EAKRING

MINE

BILSTHORPE

BILSTHORPE
TRAIL

A617

START

FARNSFIELD

PH

KIRKLINGTON

A617

SOUTHWELL TRAIL

1 MILE

they can become extremely busy; secondly, they are often in deep cuttings which, though they protect you from adverse weather, also limit views of the surrounding countryside.

This trail disgorges travellers into a new housing estate midway between old and new Bilsthorpe. Follow the road ahead to a roundabout. Take the first left into Eakring Road, signposted 'All HGVs'. Standing on a slight hill to the right of the roundabout is the old village of Bilsthorpe, part of Gilbert de Ghent's estate at the time of the Domesday Book, and worthy of a short diversion. The Saville family have held the manor since the 16th century and in the remains of the old manor house, now incorporated into the farmhouse opposite the small church of St Margaret, is a cupboard in which Charles I reputedly hid during the Civil War in the 17th century.

Returning to the route the 'new' colliery village of Bilsthorpe is soon passed, also the Bilsthorpe RUFC ground on your left and Bilsthorpe Colliery on your right. Take the first turning right after the colliery, hopefully leaving all those 'HGV's' behind, and right again at the next junction. This road to Eakring is steeply hilly, both down and up, but there are refreshments available in Eakring at The Saville Arms. If you are looking for a brief respite after the climb into the village, a stroll down the small lane beside the pub, Wellow Road, will take you to a fine old mill, minus sails. On your right, as you return to the pub, is a cottage with beautiful old decorative tiles on the roof.

Continuing through the village, take the narrow turning on the right signposted to National Grid. On your right is a village shop and on the left is the church of St Andrew. In 1669, William Mompesson was appointed rector here but the parishioners refused to let him enter the village. Four years earlier, he had been rector at Eyam when plague caused the deaths of 310 of the 350 residents. The villagers of Eakring were so frightened of contracting the plague that, for a time, William Mompesson lived in a hut in Rufford Park and preached in the open air under a tree that became known as Pulpit Ash. They did eventually relent and he stayed at Eakring for 38 years.

There is a steep pull up from the village of Eakring, with the National Grid on your left and good views over thick, protective hedges. Sherwood Forest is to your right. There is a narrow band of woodland on the right of the road, Coultas Farm on the left, then Redgate Wood on the left. Here is an optional diversion which is only suitable for the experienced off-road rider.

Off-road diversion for mountain bikers only

Turn left onto a RUPP through Redgate Wood, side tracks are private and
gated. The main track is slightly up hill but has a good surface; towards the
end of the wood are several large yews among the trees on your left. It is
unusual to find them growing wild, perhaps this was once an entrance to
Kirklington Hall, now Rodney School, at the foot of the hill. The track
suddenly swings left and continues along the east face of the wood, but you
keep straight on along a narrow bridle-path that looks more like a footpath
in a narrow band of tall shrubs and small trees between open farmland.
There is a yellow arrow here.

This is where the riding becomes exciting. Most of the path is quite firm
but there are sneaky boggy bits, branches reaching out to grab you, small
hidden tree stumps at pedal height, and slippery tree roots lying in wait for
the careless mountain biker. A footpath forks right onto farm land but the
bridle-path, continues for about half a mile. You then have to retrace your
tracks to the road through Redgate Wood.

The footpath, which is on your left as you return to the road, is part of the
Robin Hood Way and crosses a ditch on two narrow planks and continues
along the edge of the field, with the hedge and ditch on your left, towards a
small wood and some farm buildings. Here it joins a farm track and passes
to the left of the buildings, and left again beyond them. Side tracks are clearly
marked private. The track the Robin Hood Way follows, drops down
through parkland to the west of Rodney School, which celebrated 50 years
in 1994. When the track reaches the A617, it is about three quarters of a mile
into Kirklington, to the right. Turning left into Southwell Road, signposted
to both Southwell and Picnic Site, will rejoin the on-road route.

Main Route

Continue along the road past Redgate Wood and down a steep hill to the
A617, turn left and take care on this busy road. Take the first turn right with
very handsome houses on each side of the road, both with old sideways
sliding casement windows. This is Southwell Road and signposted to Southwell and Picnic Site. The two routes have now rejoined.

Take the first right signposted to Edingley and ¼ml to Picnic Site. Turn
right, before the railway bridge, to Kirklington Picnic Site on the Southwell
Trail. Turn right onto the trail and continue to the car park and picnic site at
Farnsfield.

The 'Sons and Lovers' rides:
Eastwood
and
D.H. Lawrence

The following two rides are based near Eastwood and for those interested in the author D.H. Lawrence, and with the time to spare, we recommend a two– or three-day visit to the area. With the hilly terrain this mining town is built on it would be easy to spend a whole day just visiting The D.H. Lawrence Birthplace Museum, 'Sons & Lovers' Cottage (appointment only), Beauvale Board School, etc., then a day or two cycling in the surrounding area, perhaps trying to identify places this 'poet of the landscape' put in his books. The Tourist Office has a leaflet, 'Literary Landscapes of Nottinghamshire', which gives brief details of D.H. Lawrence and others.

The first ride is a very short one along narrow ancient lanes, and would make a lovely evening ride. The second is longer, with some off-road riding. Neither are flat, both including some quite stiff, short, climbs; the second also returns to the start, at Moorgreen, via Eastwood. The two rides could be ridden in one day. The area the routes cover is in a triangle of countryside hemmed in by the M1 and the A610, but there are several bridleway bridges over the M1 which would enable more explorations of the area. To the west of Eastwood, and the A610, is the Erewash Canal which would make a great ride down to the Trent, south west of Nottingham, and along the way linking with the Strelly ride (14).

12. Beauvale

Distance:	4.5 miles
Route:	Moorgreen – Greasley – Bogend – Beauvale Priory – Moorgreen.
Surface:	Tarmac
Start:	Horse and Groom, Moorgreen. (SK485476)
Map:	O.S. Landranger 129
Parking:	The main car park behind The Horse and Groom, Moorgreen. The manager is quite happy for you to park here but do please speak to someone before leaving your vehicle for any length of time.
Accommodation:	There is B&B available in Eastwood at: 62 Garden Road, Tel. 01773 718451; The Sun Inn, Tel. 01773 712940. Unfortunately The Horse & Groom does not offer accommodation.
Comment:	This road ride is mostly on very quiet lanes, with one stiff hill.

The Journey

The main car park of The Horse & Groom is behind the pub. There is a good garden area with children's play area. Unfortunately they are not open all day. To reach the car park, approaching Moorgreen from Eastwood along the B6010, turn right onto the B600, virtually in front of The Horse & Groom, and take the first small lane to the left. The car park is on the left. Moorgreen makes a good centre for this and the following ride, which together form a contorted figure of eight.

Turn right out of the car park, then left onto the B600. This can be a surprisingly busy road so take care, but there is a little used footpath after a short distance. In about a quarter of a mile there is a church on the right, dedicated to St Mary the Virgin. It stands quite high above the road with a grey stone building called Minton's Tea Rooms beside the road. This is Greasley, called Griseleia in the Domesday Book, and though the church hiding behind handsome beech trees was largely restored in the 19th century, there was a church here in 1086 and there is a list of parish priests dating from 1254. The church contains monuments to the Rollestons of Watnall Hall, Watnall is over a mile to the south on the far side of a small valley but does not appear to have a church. Just beyond Greasley church is a farm with

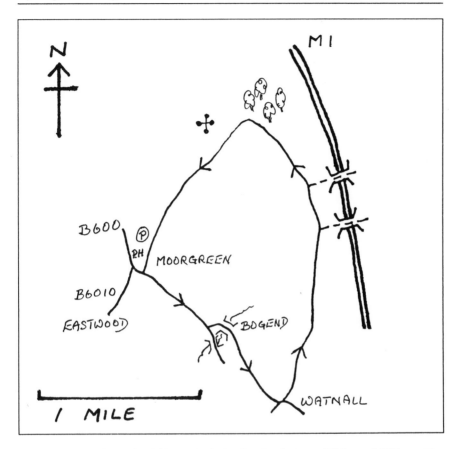

some ancient farm buildings and the banked site of Edward III's castle, which has a good view over the Erewash valley. Perhaps this tiny community was once important, as it stood in an area of desolate moorland above green valleys.

Almost opposite the site of the castle turn left into a minor lane called Church Road. This is the almost traffic-free old road, which runs parallel to the B600 but drops down to a stream and a few houses known as Bogend, before climbing steeply to Watnall. As you near the top of the hill, the roof tops of some interesting farm buildings appear over the brow on your left. At the T-junction turn left onto the B6009, called Narrow Lane, and when it bends sharp right in a few yards keep straight on into an even smaller lane with a sign saying 'No Tipping'! The farm buildings previously noted are now immediately on your left and include a fine red-brick house.

This lane is very narrow and from its sunken appearance seems extremely old. You can estimate the age by counting the number of different species in a 30-metre stretch of hedge, and multiply the number by 100 (this is known as Hooper's Rule, see *History of the Countryside* for more details). The lane passes a track to Littlefields Farm on your right and Crowhill Farm on your left. The later is also a Camping & Caravanning Club Site. On the right is a dirt racing track, either for motorbikes or go-karts, and beyond that the busy M1 lies in a deep cutting, unseen and almost unheard. There are two bridleway bridges over the motorway on your right, one leading to a minute place with the fascinating name of Chys (or is that an abbreviation?), the other leading to Hucknall.

Since climbing to Watnall, the lane has run almost along the ridge top around the head of the valley of the small stream crossed at Bogend. After a couple of right-angle bends you are cycling towards a tree-covered hilltop. As you reach the first trees, the lane swings left and you are cycling above another valley. The stream in this valley springs from a place known as Robin Hood's Well among the trees you are now leaving behind. The trees on the far side of the valley are called High Park Wood and they form a green cup in which stands the ruins of Beauvale Priory, now a farm. The priory was founded in 1343 by Nicholas de Cantelupe, a friend of Edward III. It housed an order of Carthusian monks who lived a simple life, with little contact with the rest of the world, who were great gardeners and created 'The Beautiful Valley'. Beauvale was the last priory to be founded in Nottinghamshire and only 200 years later was the first to lose its Prior in the Dissolution. Two of the priory's priors were hung at Tyburn after presenting the king with a petition and refusing to consider him head of the church.

Today, all that remain are a few ruins converted into cattle sheds and some tall, ivy clad walls with fine arched windows. By the turn of the 16th century, the valley had another link with the fight for religious freedom: John Robinson, pastor and teacher to the group of people who would become known as The Pilgrim Fathers, married a young woman from Beauvale Priory Farm at a service held in Greasley church.

On the hill on your left is Beauvale Manor Farm and you continue along the lane with the hill on the left and the valley to the right until you reach the Horse & Groom car park again.

13. Haggs Farm

Distance: 6.5 miles

Route: Moorgreen – Underwood – Eastwood – Moorgreen

Surface: Tarmac; good compacted farm tracks; rough grass tracks; dirt bridle-paths.

Start: Moorgreen (SK485476)

Map: O.S. Landranger 129 & 120

Parking: Car park of the Horse & Groom.

Accommodation: B&B in Eastwood at both The Sun Inn, Tel. 01773 712940, and 62 Garden Road, Tel. 01773 718451.

Comment: This ride takes us past the track to Haggs Farm, home of Jessie Chambers who became Miriam in 'Sons and Lovers'. The ride offers great variety both of views and terrain, from quiet woodland paths where deer may be seen, with the dark waters of a reservoir visible between the trees to steep rows of modern houses which surround the old mining town of Eastwood.

The Journey

From the car park of the Horse & Groom turn right onto the lane then right again onto the B600, passing the front entrance to the Horse & Groom on your right. The road is narrow and may be busy, so take care. You cycle downhill past houses and a turning to the left. The road swings left just after a sign warning of deer, and you turn right into a small lane then left into the private entrance to Beauvale House which is also a bridleway.

This is a good tarmac drive that winds along the edge of the woods with open glades that look perfect for deer on the right and glimpses of Moorgreen Reservoir through the trees on the left. At a fork the tarmac drive to Beauvale House continues to the right and you take the red shale bridle-path that drops downhill to the left. There is some unusual fencing on either side of this track which blends very well with the surrounding woodland and makes one think of gingerbread houses and wicked witches! The fence builder must follow the maxim 'Waste not, want not'.

Unfortunately this good track soon divides. The good section dropping downhill is a footpath, while the bridle-path continues on a higher level, with a poor surface. Before long a wide limestone track can be seen through the shrubs on your right, if you can get through to it the riding will be much

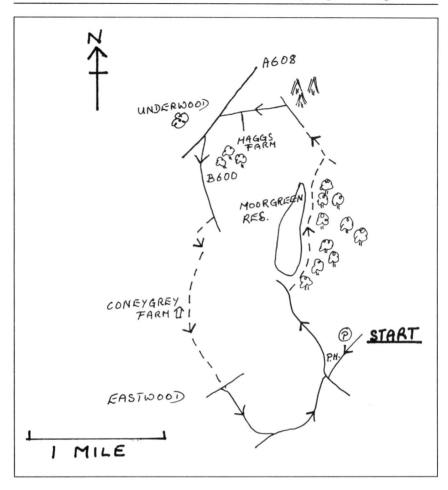

easier. The bridle-path eventually joins this track which soon becomes a lane with a steep hill ahead. Do not climb that hill but turn left onto another lane opposite a brick pill box, left over from the second World War. Don't imagine you have avoided hill work, there is a steep one ahead! As you climb you will pass the entrance to Haggs Farm on your left. This is where D.H. Lawrence spent a great deal of time when he was recovering from a near fatal bout of pneumonia at the age of fifteen in 1901.

Turn left onto the A608 at the top of the hill, then first left again onto the B600. It is a shame to have to dice with traffic again but it is only briefly as you turn right onto the short stretch of concrete track to Willey Wood Farm, signposted as a bridleway. Do not turn right up the farm entrance, but keep straight on, then bear left along a wide vehicle track across the fields. Eastwood, the valley of the Erewash (river and canal), and Derbyshire are ahead. Passing through a gate you follow the track down towards Coney-grey Farm. Close to the farm house and buildings go through a gate onto a wide, mown strip of grass which passes behind the house (with it on your right), and through another gate onto the farm drive.

The name of this farm gives a strong clue to its ancient origins. In Medieval England, the Lord of the Manor usually kept a rabbit warren which, with the dovecote, supplied fresh meat for his table, even in winter. The warren was an important part of the estate and this lovely old substantial farmhouse reinforces this point.

Turn left in the farm entrance, cross the cattle grid and follow the farm drive downhill, do not take the bridle-path which turns off right, but continue to the tarmac road. Turn right onto the tarmac road then immediately left into Mill Road. You are on the outskirts of Eastwood and Mill Road is a long steep climb. At the top, turn left at the T-junction, signposted to Moorgreen. If you wish to visit the museum you will need to turn right and right again into the town centre.

Continuing with the ride you pass through Beauvale with the Ram Inn on your left and continue downhill to The Horse & Groom, where you turn right onto the B600. Turn first left and the car park is on your left.

14. Cossall

Distance:	5 miles
Route:	Strelley – Awsworth – Cossall Marsh – Cossall – Strelley
Surface:	Good compacted tracks, tarmac, some rough bridle-paths.
Start:	Strelley (SK505422)
Map:	O.S. Landranger 129
Parking:	Very limited but a little room through the five-barred gate at the start of the ride, or ask permission at The Broad Oak public house, Strelley.
Accommodation:	There is accommodation in Cossall at Chatterley House Hotel, Tel. 0115 930 4519 and The Haven, Tel. 0115 930 7924. This ride is easily reached from Nottingham City Centre (either by car or bike) where there is an abundance of accommodation, contact Nottingham Tourist Office for details, Tel. 0115 947 0661.
Comment:	This is a very peaceful ride, despite the nearness of Nottingham and the M1. It is mostly off-road, though some vehicles do use the tracks, so take care. There is one 'A' road to be crossed twice, and two short stretches of minor road. There are links with D.H. Lawrence: Cossall village is the setting for The Rainbow, and the village of Strelley has been owned by only two families (Strelley and Edge) since Norman times.

The Journey

Strelley is approached from the busy A6002, which forms the western boundary of Nottingham City and its satellite urban areas, down a lane signposted 'No Through Road', and shaded by tall old trees. As you cycle down this road, The Broad Oak is on the right, as is the Hall and its grounds, rebuilt in 1789, and the church. The entry in the Domesday Book reads, 'Straelie/Straleia; Godwin the priest and Ambrose from William Peverel; Wulfsi and Godwin from the king', but by the 12th century the resident lord of the manor had taken the name Strelley and they were to remain lords of the manor for about five hundred years, until the estate passed into the hands of a family called Edge, who are still living here. The church of All Saints contains memorials to many Strelleys, including Sir Robert who fought with his king, Henry V, at the battle of Agincourt in 1415.

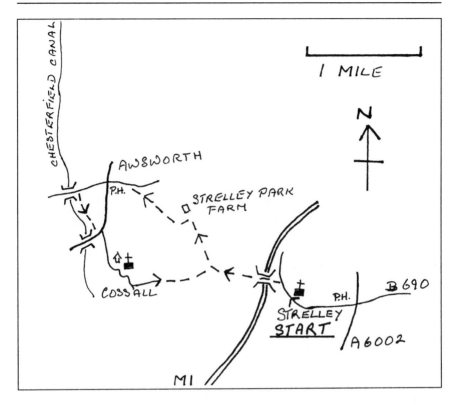

Shortly after passing the church there is a new wooden fence and a very large gate on the left. This gate has a chain and padlock which seem not to be used, but there is a bridleway entrance to the right of the gate. There is room to park a car through the gate if you have arrived by vehicle. Through the gateway keep to the right where a hedged, stony track (keep an ear open for vehicles) rises to a bridge over the M1. This noisy road is in a deep gully which contains the sound and can soon be forgotten as you cycle into an area of hedgerows and open arable land.

When the track bends right towards Turkey Fields Farm, a narrow, signed, bridle-path continues straight ahead. This path, which runs down the edge of a field, appears to have been a tarmac lane but is now badly eroded. The views towards Cossall and Derbyshire pass you by as you study the ground for the easiest, safest route.

When the path rejoins the track, keep straight ahead. Again at the next junction, where there is a large pile of unused tarmac on the right, keep

Cossall Alms Houses, founded in 1685

straight ahead. Apart from the bridle-path the surface on these old lanes is very good. When you reach a T-junction, with the entrance drive to Strelley Park Farm straight ahead, turn left and follow the bridleway, until you meet a tarmac lane. Keep straight ahead on this lane which almost immediately bends sharp left and climbs a hill to the A6096 at Awsworth, another of William Peverel's possessions in 1086. There is a pub on the left at this junction.

Cross straight over the A6096, which can be quite difficult unless some kind driver waits for you, continues through the houses and then drops down into the Erewash Valley. In the valley bottom is the River Erewash which forms the boundary between Nottinghamshire and Derbyshire. Beyond the river is the Erewash Canal; the tow path of this canal can be followed south all the way to Trentlock. Turn left into a very wide cinder entrance just before the disused Nottingham Canal with a bridleway sign.

You will catch a glimpse of the canal immediately on your right before the track passes in front of some buildings and appears to enter a scrap yard! There is a scrap yard here but also several other firms, watch out for guard dogs, all chained hopefully. Keep straight ahead until you reach the 'Pallet' firm. Bear right in front of their fence onto a horrible looking wet track. This is a little overgrown but not too bad and rapidly improves as the canal appears on your right. Where there is a wooden footbridge over the canal, do not cross the bridge, follow the narrow bridle-path to the left. Follow the fenced path around a field, swinging right in the far corner and heading down towards the houses of Cossall Marsh where you follow the path to the A6096.

The route crosses straight over into Church Lane, but this crossing is on a slight bend in the road with poor vision it may be prudent to cycle a few yards to the left before crossing. Church Lane is a steep road climbing to Cossall, though it is a minor road it does link two 'A' roads and may be busy. Keep well away from the high kerbstones.

D.H. Lawrence used Cossall as the setting for his book The Rainbow, calling it Cossethay, which was first published in 1915 and seized by the authorities who declared it obscene. In 1086 the place was known as Coteshale and, like most of the area, held by William Peverel. It is also the place where the first coal was dug in Nottinghamshire over seven centuries ago. What would those miners say about the present situation?

The road runs into Cossall and swings sharp left. On your left is a row of almshouses built by George Willoughby in 1685. Beyond them is the village hall and, beyond that, a pretty cottage. This was the home of Louie Burrows in 1910 when she became engaged to D.H. Lawrence, and is also 'Yew Cottage', home of Will and Anna Brangwen in The Rainbow. All that seems to have changed is that the slate roof has been replaced by red pantiles with just a few rows of slates peeping out from the eaves. The church has been mostly rebuilt, in the mid-1800s, but contains a few interesting memorials and some excellent carving done by villagers.

Follow the road through the village past the church and when it bends sharp right, keep straight on to a 'No Through Road' signposted as a Bridleway to Strelley. You will eventually reach a T-junction which you should recognise – ahead is that heap of old tarmac seen earlier! Turn right here and retrace your tracks, keeping straight on into the narrow bridle-path, keep your curses to yourself as you negotiate those tarmac steps in low gear, uphill this time, then rejoin the good track that takes you over all those buzzing vehicles on the M1, then down into Strelley again and the end of the journey.

15. Blidworth &
Papplewick Pumping station

Distance: 8 miles

Route: Blidworth Wood – Blidworth – Papplewick Pumping Station – Blidworth Wood.

Surface: Tarmac, plus short section of narrow, dirt bridle-path.

Start: Blidworth Wood Western Car Park and Picnic Site (SK584532)

Map: O.S. Landranger 120

Parking: Blidworth Wood Western Car Park, Rigg Lane

Accommodation: B&B available at Forest Farm, Papplewick, Tel. 0115 963 2310, and The Willow Tree, Papplewick, Tel. 0115 963 2642, or Holly Lodge, Blidworth, Tel. 01623 793853.

Comment: This is another 'Robin Hood' ride through an area that was part of the Royal Forest hunting grounds. Blidworth Woods is a small patch of woodland surrounded by modern coal mining areas, yet the ride takes us through beautiful rural countryside. There are three car parks in Blidworth Woods; we have chosen the western one as it is on the route of the ride. Do remember the compass for forest riding and only ride on hard roads and tracks, preferably avoiding those used heavily by walkers. This ride has several steep hills, allow plenty of time.

The Journey

The Car Park & Picnic Site on Rigg Lane is just north of Blidworth Lodge, if you are approaching from the south. You could cycle through the forest to the car park at Blidworth Bottoms then turn left onto the road, rejoining the following route at the foot of Rigg Lane by the pub.

From the car park (on Rigg Lane) turn right onto the lane. This is quite narrow and you may have to get off the road to allow traffic to pass but it is very quiet. There is a great run down to a T-junction and a pub at Blidworth Bottoms. Turn left at the T-junction then immediately right and begin the first of several steep climbs.

At the top turn left onto the B6020 and into the old village of Blidworth and perhaps a welcome rest at The Black Bull. To the right is the modern mining village. The old village stands on a ridge that must have given

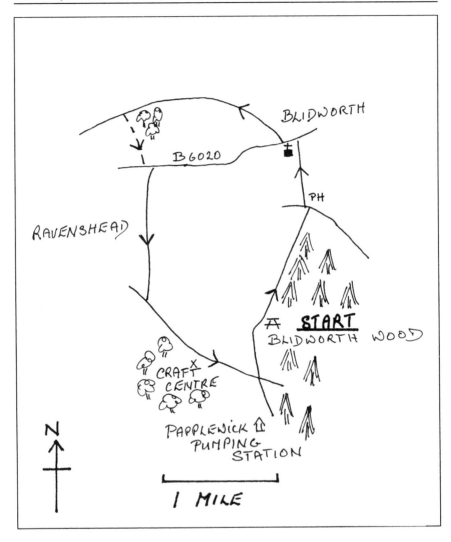

excellent views over the surrounding forest of Sherwood; on a clear day you can see the spire of Newark, the towers of Lincoln Cathedral, and Belvoir Castle. Blidworth is reputed to be the home of Maid Marion and she may have been married here in the church where Will Scarlet is believed to be buried. Blidworth was the home of some of the Forest Rangers, Robin Hood's enemies, and the church contains a memorial to one, Thomas Leake, which has carvings of hunting horns, longbows and hounds.

Blidworth has strong Robin Hood connections

The route continues by turning right, off the B6020 just beyond the church, into Rickett Lane which climbs out of the village into open countryside full of horses. Every field seems to contain horses, chestnuts, greys, palominos. The lane drops downhill but is essentially a ridgeway route with ancient hedges and fields dropping steeply away to the left.

When you reach a wood on your left note the Scout Camp sign (and the Keep Out signs). Just beyond the Scout Camp, and before a house hidden in the woods, is a narrow signed bridle-path on your left. The entrance to the path is quite steep and with plenty of tree roots to catch the unwary, we would advise walking a short distance at least. Using this bridle-path avoids a section of busy A-road. On the map the route is straight downhill but you will find yourself twisting and turning to avoid the grasping spikes of gorse bushes.

At the bottom turn left onto the B6020 and first right into Chapel Lane, another stiff climb, with Ravenshead to your right. Beyond Ravenshead is Newstead Abbey, home of Lord Byron, which should be worth a visit if you are staying in the area. The lane reaches a T-junction where you turn left onto Long Dale Lane. In about three quarters of a mile the Longdale Craft Centre Museum & Restaurant are on the right. Beyond here is a crossroads. The end of the ride is to the left but to the right is Papplewick Pumping Station, an ornate Victorian waterworks which is open from 2pm to 5pm from Easter to October. For details of special Steaming Days, Tel. 0115 963 2938. The station is less than a quarter of a mile down this small lane on the right. After visiting it return to the crossroads, cross straight over into Rigg Lane which climbs to Blidworth Lodge, then just round the bend is the car park and picnic site from which you started.

16. Epperstone & Lambley

Distance:	12.5 miles
Route:	Grimesmoor – Woodborough – Lambley – Lowdham – Epperstone – Grimesmoor.
Surface:	Tarmac, dirt bridle-path and track
Start:	Grimesmoor Camping and Caravanning Site (SK634489)
Map:	O.S. Landranger 129
Parking:	If not camping, the campsite at Grimesmoor *may* give permission to use their car park, or you can start the ride in Epperstone which has wide grass verges along the road to Gonalston.
Accommodation:	There is a campsite at Grimesmoor which has a fishing lake and many residential vans; it is not unattractive but the washing facilities are poor. There is also Moor Farm Trailer Park (Tel. 0115 965 2426); B&B at Patchings Farm Cottage, Calverton (Tel. 0115 965 3479) which is also an Art Centre with a working art and pottery studio; Hall Farm House, Gonalston (Tel. 0115 966 3112).
Comment:	This is a very hilly ride through some beautiful countryside just north east of Nottingham City. The area is steeped in history including a squabble between Woodborough and Calverton over which is the birthplace of William Lee, the inventor of the 'stocking frame', which revolutionised the knitting industry. The route is mainly on road with a short section of rough bridle-path, a section of 'white road' used by tracked vehicles, and one of the loveliest bridle-paths in Nottinghamshire through the grounds of an old mill.

The Journey

The ride begins at the Grimesmoor Camping and Caravanning Site on the lane from the A6097 to Calverton. The site is signed on the main road. This is the only camp site we have visited where one has needed to undress virtually in public before taking a shower! Fortunately most caravanners have their own toilet facilities and the toilet block is mostly empty. Turn left out of the site, opposite there is a restaurant and a little further along the road is the Club House and Chinese Restaurant of the Golf Club which forms the backdrop to the campsite.

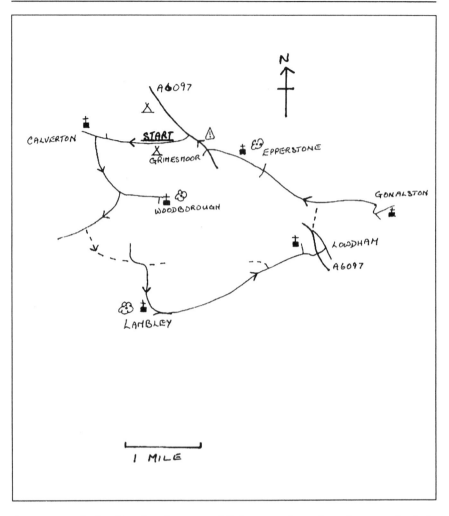

As you reach the first few houses of Calverton there is a shop on the left, almost immediately the route turns left into Banner Hill. Calverton is well worth a short visit if only to see the Calverton Folk Museum housed in a small stocking-maker's cottage in the main street. The Museum is only open by appointment, Tel. 0115 965 2836. William Lee invented the stocking frame during the reign of Elizabeth I but she refused a patent, partly because it did not make silk stockings. When William solved this problem, she realised it would put huge numbers of people out of work. William then took his invention to France where Henry IV promised his patronage, but unfortunately he was assassinated and William was left to die, penniless in Paris in 1610.

Returning to the route you start up Banner Hill, a steep, stiff climb before a pleasant run down into Woodborough. Both Roger de Bully and the Archbishop of York, who also owned land in Calverton, had estates here in 'Udesburg' in 1086. The village is an attractive place with tall trees shading the main street. Continue along the main street to visit St Swithin's Church on the right and almost opposite The Four Bells. This name is very appropriate as the church, which was partly built by Richard Strelley who lived in the village in the 14th century, has a tradition of ringing the church bells on Shrove Tuesday when it is time for the housewives of the village to mix the batter for the pancakes!

An inviting hostelry opposite the church in Woodborugh

Retrace your tracks along the main street to a turning on the left signposted to Arnold, and called Bank Hill. You guessed it, you are in for another climb, slightly easier this time as the road tries to follow the contours. On your left as you turn into this road is Woodborough Hall, probably the site of Richard Strelley's home but now a Nursing Home. After leaving the village this is a long steady climb with excellent views. Just after passing the entrance to a property called High Pastures, in a tall hedge, under low hanging trees, there is a signed bridle-path on the left. This is a fairly narrow bridle-path with a hedge on the right and fence on the left. Keep straight ahead when a green track crosses the bridle-path coming from the farm buildings on your right. Beyond here there are stinging nettles bordering the path as it drops down, then climbs to a wide dirt track, which is the white road from Lambley House on the O.S. map.

Turn left onto this track which is quite soft and peaty in places, well-broken by tractors. The surface improves, which leaves you free to take in the magnificent views across to the valleys of the Dover Beck and the Trent. You are crossing Hunger Hill (there must be a story in a name like that), and eventually rejoin the tarmac high above the village of Lambley. Keep straight ahead when you join the road and, when it bends right, there is an optional off-road section on the left along a signed bridleway which would miss out Lambley and take you cross-country to Lowdham.

However, the main route continues downhill into the village. Take great care – this is extremely steep. The road swings left at the bottom and, a little further on, the church of The Holy Trinity is on your right. Lambley is the birthplace of Ralph, Lord Cromwell, born 1394 and the last of ten generations to bear the name. He became High Treasurer of England in 1433 and built Lincolnshire's Tattershall Castle. He also made alterations to Lambley church and his badge of office, a purse, can be found, carved in stone, by those with sharp eyes.

Turn left beyond the church at a T-junction, to Lowdham, with the Cocker Beck on your left. The road follows the Beck along the valley and just before reaching Lowdham those who took the off-road route will rejoin us near the entrance to Lowdham Grange. Continue into Lowdham and take the first small lane to the left which will lead you to Lowdham Church set in a lovely glade with Cocker Beck running by and containing the image of Sir John de Lowdham, a knight in chain mail and holding a shield.

Return to the road which swings right then sharp left before reaching traffic lights on the A6097 dual-carriageway. Cross straight over, on the green light, into a shady lane leading to the rest of Lowdham. At a T-junction turn left, away from the main village, and continue until this road meets the A6097. Do not go onto the main road but turn right onto a tarmac track beside it, then almost immediately right again into the entrance drive to Lowdham Mill with a turf field on the left of the drive.

Down the drive there is a gateway to the mill and on the right a wicket gate onto a beautifully mown grass path under some trees, this path is the bridle-path, which skirts the garden of the watermill before crossing a couple of fields and Dover Beck and then reaching a tarmac lane. The route turns left onto this lane but to the right is the village of Gonalston, an attractive village, worth at least a short visit.

Like most of the villages on this ride, Gonalston had a couple of mills at the time of the Domesday Book. In many of these mills, until as late as the 19th century, child slaves laboured from the age of about seven for fourteen or sixteen hours a day, often until they died (at a very early age).

Returning to the ride the route heads north west for Epperstone, home of the Howe family (no relation), where a small H over the gate of the Manor House (now a unit of the Nottinghamshire Police Force) is almost the only reference to a family who owned it for many years. In the Domesday Book, there were several mills here in 1086. One was a paper mill which was still functioning in 1723 and eventually made wads for the muzzle-loading guns used during the Crimean War and the Indian Mutiny. The church is one of 83 in the country dedicated to The Holy Cross and stands on a rise on the right of the road.

Continue through the village until you meet the A6097. Turn right onto this road and cycle with great care for about a quarter of a mile. Take the second left turning, signposted to Calverton and Camp Site, and return to the Grimesmoor campsite and the end of the ride.

17. Kneesall

Distance: 9 miles
Route: Kneesall – Maplebeck – Kersall – Kneesall
Surface: Tarmac
Start: Kneesall (SK704641)
Map: O.S. Landranger 120
Parking: Around the village green.
Accommodation: There is self-catering accommodation in Kneesall and Kersall, and a guest house in Kersall. For details, Tel. 01636 78962.
Comment: A ride around a small part of Gilbert de Ghent's estate (1086). When William the Conqueror became King of England he set his scribes the task of making an inventory of the whole country, village by village. The Domesday Book was the result. From this great and unique 900-year-old book you can discover the general size of individual villages, details of mills and manor houses, and which of William's knights had acquired the ownership of the area. All three of the villages on this ride were in the ownership of Gilbert de Ghent in 1086. You can imagine, as you progress from village to village that you might be one of those same scribes, noting all the details for presentation to your King. The ride includes a couple of steep hills.

The Journey

This ride starts in School Lane, Kneesall, under the gaze of grotesque gargoyles on the 15th century tower of the church of St Bartholomew. Turn right onto the A616 and in about 100 yards turn left, signposted to Eakring, in front of a magnificent old house, reputed to be one of the earliest brick houses in the county. It is so eyecatching that we cycled straight past the turning on our first visit to this area, so be warned! There is a pleasant downhill stretch. At the T-junction turn left, signposted to Caunton.

The road soon drops down to run gently along beside The Beck. Don't be misled, as this ride is meant to test your lungs. Take the first turning right, signposted to Maplebeck, and immediately there is a short stiff climb to the top of the village, and an equally steep drop down. On your right is The Beehive, built in 1803 and reputedly one of the smallest pubs in the country.

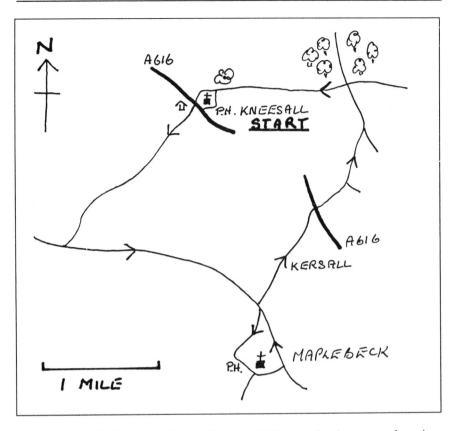

The church of St Radegund, standing on a hill opposite, is very welcoming, with a smiling face on an ancient beam in the porch that is probably over 600 years old. Many people have caressed that face as they entered and his features have almost disappeared. St Radegund was a German princess of the 6th century, abducted by a French King, who sought safety at Poitiers where she founded a convent. The church was built at the end of the 12th century and now stands on its small hill surrounded by beautiful trees which include an ancient yew from which bows were made for the Battle of Agincourt (1415) and a rare and unusual Tulip Tree, which bears yellow flowers.

In 1251, the village was owned by the Cistercian monks of Rufford Abbey, though the church belonged first to the Knights Templars, and then the Knights Hospitaller. By the 19th century, both village and church were owned by Lord Middleton, who lost the lot during an evening's gambling to the then Earl Fitzwilliam, whose descendants are still St Radegund's patrons.

The ride continues past the church through the village to a T-junction. Turn left, signposted to Eakring, and follow the road around the base of the hill that Maplebeck stands on. Take the first turning right, signposted to Kersall, cross The Beck and immediately begin a 12% climb into the tiny village of Kersall. In the 16th and 17th centuries this was a Quaker village; now, it boasts the Best Kept Phone Box in the World!

Continue through the village to the A616, cross straight over, signposted to Laxton. Ignore side roads and continue to a crossroads, turn left towards Kneesall along an unfenced road. The land to your right is part of Laxton's medieval open field farm land. Turn left into School Lane, Kneesall, and you are back where you started.

18. Winkburn

Distance:	10 miles
Route:	Caunton – Maplebeck – Winkburn – Hockerton – Caunton
Surface:	Tarmac
Start:	Caunton (SK746601)
Map:	O.S. Landranger 120
Parking:	There is a layby on the A616 on the outskirts of Caunton, or The Plough Pub opposite the church in the centre of the village, but don't forget to ask for permission to park.

Accommodation: For B&B in Caunton, Tel. 01636 86729

Comment: This is a pleasant village ride which includes hills, views, ancient churches, and about a mile on the A617.

The Journey

The ride begins in the village of Caunton a pretty village with a stream running through the centre, shaded by willows along the edge of the church yard where ducks beg for the odd crust. Beside the stream is possibly the most handsome bus shelter in the county, but buses may be thin on the ground these days. The Plough Pub, which is an attractive and hospitable hostelry serving food and allowing children in for meals, lies west of St Andrew's Church. To the south of the church is an old hostelry called The Hole, which now is closed and in a sad state of decay. It is named after the Hole family who lived at the manor across the road, from the 15th century. This was where the man Tennyson dubbed 'The Rose King' spent most of his life. Samuel Hole, who died in 1904, loved roses; he studied them, grew them, wrote about them, he was even instrumental in the formation of The National Rose Society. So perhaps you should not be surprised that many gardens in the area are so beautiful.

From the churchyard cross the stream and turn right into Manor Road. Turn right onto the A616 (there is a layby on your right), signposted to Sheffield. Take the first left, signposted to Maplebeck, a small lane which drops gently down to the valley of The Beck, the stream which runs through Caunton, with Beesthorpe Hall on the far side of the valley. Take the first turning left, signposted to Maplebeck.

Maplebeck is much smaller than Caunton and has the distinction of having the smallest Inn in the county, the Beehive. On the small hill opposite

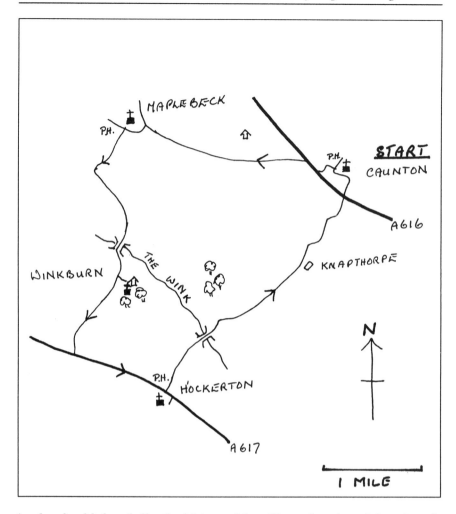

is a lovely old church (for the history of the village, church and churchyard, see page 81).

Continuing the ride, take the lane opposite the church, signposted to Winkburn. There is a hard pull up to Maplebeck View Point where a seat is thoughtfully placed, then a gentle drop down to the River Wink and then the village of Winkburn. When the road through the village makes a sharp right bend turn left into a short 'no through' road which leads to the entrance to Winkburn Hall. Here a charming notice warns that there is only footpath access to the church along the 'Carriage Way' through the Hall's private land. The four-square Hall is mostly 18th century and a very handsome building in its day, it is currently being restored and may be open to the public. The church which stands to the right of the Hall, almost hidden by trees, is Norman.

The Church of St John of Jerusalem, and the village of Wynkebourne (as it was known then) were presented to the Knights Hospitaller in the twelfth century. The path to the church crosses a small bridge over what may be the remains of a moat which probably surrounded the church and original house where the Knights and priests lived. Windows on the church tower are embellished with both zigzag and cable Norman carving, and there are beak-heads around the high doorway. Inside are uncomfortable looking box pews, each with its own door, and many with several layers of carpet on the stone flags. It is fun to sit in one of these boxes and imagine a large family filling it, with Mum and Dad facing the handsome three-decker pulpit and the children, with their backs to the preacher, hardly daring to move under their fathers wrathful glare.

Return to the road through the village, turning left onto it and cycling along a pleasant road through parkland with magnificent trees and a herd of ponies that could be Dartmoors. Reaching the A617 turn left, signposted to Newark. This is a busy road, so take care for the next mile.

At Hockerton turn left, signposted to Caunton, beside The Spread Eagle public house. There is a short climb before the road drops down to the River Wink and then climbs gently up the far side of the valley. On reaching the A616 cross straight over for Caunton and the end of the ride.

19. Blyth

Distance: 14 miles

Route: Blyth – Hodstock – Oldcotes – Styrrup – Serlby – Blyth

Surface: Tarmac, a variety of compacted surfaces such as cinder & soil, dirt & grass bridle-paths.

Start: Blyth village centre (SK625870)

Map: O.S. Landranger 111

Parking: The car park outside The White Swan is a public car park.

Accommodation: B&B is available at both The Fourways Hotel, Tel. 01909 591235 in the very centre of Blyth, and The Angel Inn, Tel. 01909 591213 reputedly dating from 1274 when Knights and their retinues stayed here before jousting tournaments and which had a tunnel linking it to the priory.

Comment: This ride will take us back to '1066 and all that'. Blyth was the centre of Roger de Bully's estates in the 11th century. Very little is known about Roger de Bully though he probably came from Busli, near Rouen, in Normandy. He was granted huge areas of land when William the Conqueror laid waste the north of England after the inhabitants rebelled, so perhaps he helped to subdue the natives! He built a castle here in Blyth, which has completely disappeared, and gave land to the Benedictine monks who began to build a priory in 1088, of which only a small part remains in the fabric of the church of St Mary and St Martin.

The Great North Road ran straight through the centre of Blyth until recent years when the village was by-passed, and one of its claims to fame this century is as the centre of the Time Trial world. Time Trials still take place on parts of the Great North Road but the days when hundreds of cyclists gathered in the centre of this pleasant small town have gone, as have the many cafes that served them. Hodsock Priory garden is open to the public, for details, Tel. 01909 591204.

The Journey

The day's ride begins in the town centre where you take the B6045 almost opposite The White Swan. This is the road to Worksop and may be quite

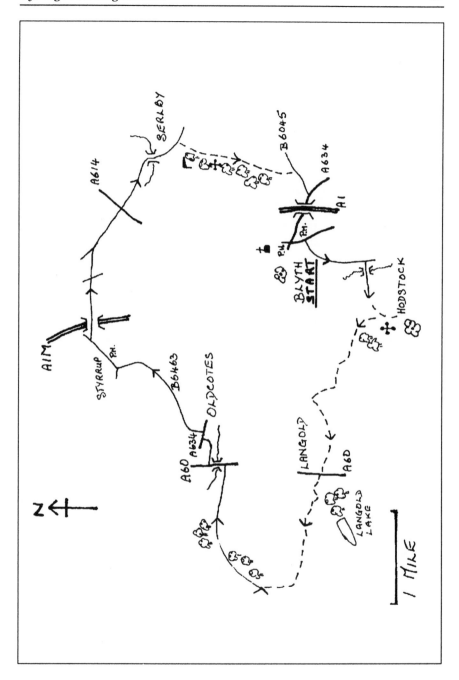

busy at times. The road climbs out of Blyth then begins to drop down into the valley of the River Ryton. Turn right into a narrow shaded lane signposted to Hodsock Priory and Hodsock Priory Guest House. The lane crosses the River Ryton, passes some cottages and enters parkland over a cattle-grid. Now you begin to feel like a knight riding through your domain, and you may well see several beautiful horses as there are stables at Hodsock. As the drive swings left you see ahead the magnificent Tudor gateway to Hodsock Priory which was the home of the Cressy's and the Clifton's. The gardens of Hodsock Priory are open to the public every Sunday from Easter to the second Sunday in July, from 2pm – 5pm. The house is not open but can be viewed from the garden which opens also in February and March for the annual Snowdrop Spectaculars.

To the right a green track crosses the open land to double gates into a field. Continue across the field with the wood on your left, to the far left-hand corner. Here there are two gates one in front of you, one to the left, take the iron gate on your left leading to a track along the edge of the wood.

Keep straight ahead, crossing straight over a woodchip gallop and following the track to Hodsock Lodge Farm, also stables. Follow the track to the right around the farm buildings and join their lane turning right onto it and follow this drive to a crossroads. Opposite is the drive to Hodsock Park and yet more magnificent horses. Turn left at this crossroads and follow the unfenced lane through arable land to the A60.

Cross straight over the A60 into Langold Country Park and from the car park follow a cinder path to the right around the grass area. Keep to the left of the swings and follow into trees on the opposite side of the grass. Here you have a choice: either follow the path to a T-junction on the far side of the wood and turn right to leave the park, or follow the blue arrows to the left which take you up onto a ridged track. This is used by mountain bikers and leads to another car park with a lake to the left. Turn right and cycle through the car park and leave Langold Park through a gateway. The routes have now converged.

Turn left out of the park onto a cinder vehicle track. This track climbs steadily, and somewhere along here crosses the boundary into South Yorkshire. At a crossroads of tracks keep straight on, signposted bridleway (there is also a bridleway to the right which you do not take as the track deteriorates into a poor grass track). Continue straight ahead then follow the lane right to the B6463. Turn right and follow this road as it heads back into Nottinghamshire and down to the A60. This is the Worksop to Doncaster road and could be busy, so take care. The road drops downhill, crosses a small stream and begins to climb to a junction. Take the first turning to the right after the stream, called Main Street, and cycle through the attractive village of Old-cotes, following the road as it swings left to the A634.

The embattled Tudor gateway to Hodsock Priory

Turn right onto the A634, then left onto the B6463 beside the magnificent brick buildings and house of Manor Farm. You are heading for a place called Styrrup and over to the right is the site of one of England's five Tournament Fields during the reign of Richard I. Here in 1194, in fields now known as Terminings Meadow (from the word tourneying), Raker Field (from wrecker or combatant), and Gallant Steads enclosure, the knights and their retinues gathered to display and test their fighting skills watched by crowds of spectators jostling for a good vantage point on a nearby mound. The village of Styrrup must be named after these exciting gatherings, maybe one party camped here and another nearer to Blyth which is only a couple of miles away as the crow flies, or the horse gallops.

The road runs into Styrrup which is an attractive village that has seen some redevelopment of the old farm buildings that line the main street. Almost opposite the old hall, turn right into Serlby Road, signposted to Serlby. This road climbs quite steeply and bridges the A1(M) before dropping down, with an old coal spoil tip on your right, to a crossroads. Straight over the crossroads, there are spoil tips both sides of the road, and continue to a T-junction. Turn right, signposted to Serlby, and continue to the A614. Cross straight over into a road through Serlby Park. In 1086 this was called Serlebi and was part of Roger de Bully's estate. Today, there are race horses, a golf course and the handsome house that stands on the hill ahead and to the right. Stay on the main lane that passes the entrance to the Hall, crosses the River Ryton and swings right to pass the golf course and club house on your right and leave the park through another gateway beside a lodge house.

Immediately after the lodge turn right onto a bridleway that runs along the course of a bank known as Roman Bank with the golf course on your right. This is a lovely path with handsome spreading beech trees on the right and open farmland on the left. The path crosses straight over another track, continuing along the line of the Roman Bank with a thick wood on the right, until it reaches the B6045. Turn right onto this road, and right again when you reach the A634 which passes under the A1 and enters Blyth. Turn left in the village centre for the White Swan and the end of the ride.

20. Pleasley Trails – Part 1

Distance: 10 miles

Route: Pleasley – Teversal – Skegby – Pleasley

Surface: Good compacted paths, a variety of cinder, stone, and dirt.

Start: Outgang Road Car Park, Pleasley Vale. (SK509649)

Map: O.S. Landranger 120 & Pleasley Trails Network leaflet available from Ashfield District Council, Tel. Mansfield 755755

Parking: Outgang Road Car Park.

Accommodation: There is a variety of accommodation in Mansfield and Sutton in Ashfield; for details contact Nottinghamshire County Council, Tel. 0115 977 4212. In Skegby, there is Dalestorth Guesthouse – Tel. 01623 551110.

Comment: This ride and the following short one are two pleasant off-road rides suitable for family groups, passing through a variety of habitats. The only unpleasant surprises are a couple of stiles to be negotiated and a couple of steep banks where the trail crosses minor lanes.

To reach the car park on Outgang Road, turn off the A617 at the Pleasley roundabout onto the B6407, signposted to Shirebrook, then immediately right onto a small lane, signposted to Pleasley Vale. The car park is on the right in about half a mile. This network of trails follows old railway tracks which carried coal from the surrounding collieries. The first line was opened in 1866 and the last line was closed in 1968, just over one hundred years of commercial service.

The Journey

From Outgang Car Park, follow the path that runs to the south west towards Pleasley, and drops down to the River Meden. Cross the river and turn right onto the path. This is a heavily walked area, so please cycle at a gentle speed and let walkers know of your approach. If you are using the Pleasley Network Trail leaflet you will notice a discrepancy here, it shows the path on the north of the river but it is on the south bank. Just before the path reaches a major road turn right on the path that takes you under the road and runs beside the river to the main street of Pleasley. The end of this path bears a footpath sign. When you reach the road there is a Post Office and Store on your left.

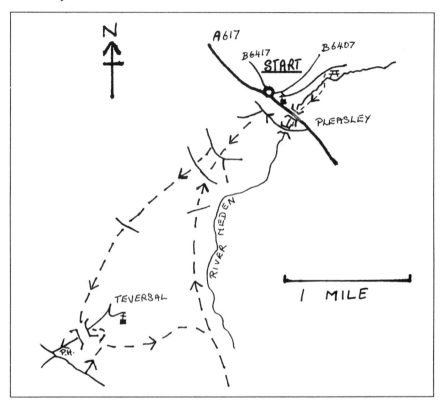

Turn right onto the road, Chesterfield Road, and cycle up the hill. When you reach the Pleasley Surgery on your right turn left onto an un-named road (we believe it is called Pit Lane). On your left, shortly, is the start of the main Teversal Trail with a difficult narrow access point beside a five-bar wooden gate. The surface is good and there is an abundance of wild flowers. At once you have left the world of commerce and housing estates behind. Honeysuckle cascades down the right-hand bank and beyond the stinging nettles you find a carpet of interesting flowers.

The trail continues through a deep cutting between sheer red rock walls, climbs steeply up to Longhedge Lane Bridleway where you turn right and follow the bridleway for a short distance. The original trail does continue straight on at Longhedge Lane but we recommend following the circular route in an anti-clockwise direction and travelling south on the yellow Teversal Trail, then north on the red Teversal Trail. There are two reasons for this: 1. It makes the short road section at Teversal much safer. 2. There are some difficult stiles to cross and steps to negotiate along the yellow route which are best handled while you are fresh! If, after tackling them, you feel these are inappropriate barriers on a family trail, contact Ashfield District Council Community Services (Leisure) Tel. 01623 755755

Having turned right onto Longhedge Lane from the first section of the trail continue with some old spoil tips on your right for about a hundred yards or so, then left through a narrow gap in the wooden fence and down a steep bank to the yellow Teversal Trail, another old railway track. The surface of this bank is very loose take care especially if you are accompanied by young children. We also feel the entrances to these trails are too narrow though we do appreciate they are intended to keep motor cyclists out.

You may notice short posts at strategic spots around the trail that look as if they should bear signs or some form of information. At the time of writing they do not. It would be very helpful if they did!

The trail continues along the track through a wide cutting. The sparse vegetation suggests calcareous grasslands and there may be some interesting plants here, particularly grasses. Then the trail is on higher land than the surroundings and there are wide views of folding hills and distant farmsteads. Along here the route re-enters Nottinghamshire and also becomes a deep cutting again. At Newbound Lane there is another steep climb to the road and a stile out onto it, then another to rejoin the trail. There is only one more stile and, however annoying they are, the cycling is worth the effort.

The trail now enters an area of crowding scrub as it approaches Teversal. When a proper (though we think unused) railway track joins the trail from the right both track and trail cross a bridge over a road and then there is the last of the stiles. Once negotiated there is another obstacle to surprise you. On the left is a flight of steps down to the road. Don't get out of control!

When you reach the road you may wish to take a short diversion to the right into the old village of Teversal, once the home of the Molyneux family, but the route turns left onto the road and continues under the three 'side by side' bridges. Cycle along this lane, then turn left onto the B6014 beside a large inviting public house. For those more interested in a refreshing cup of tea there are refreshments available shortly at the Visitor Centre. The B6014 runs downhill, under a railway bridge and between modern colliery housing. Take the first turning on the left, signposted to the Social Club. The Teversal Visitor Centre is on the left at the car park. There are light refreshments available and the staff are very helpful. They may also have leaflets on cycleways, footpaths, and bridleways in the area.

The route continues through the car park, through the cycle gateway, much easier thank goodness, and right onto the trail. Here is a very different area. The land slopes gently away to the left and right with several rows of trees standing in lush green grass and concealing any view. Again the surroundings vary between deep cuttings and banks high above the sur-roundings. One minute you are in a cocoon-like world of your own, the next it seems you are on top of the world with agricultural Nottinghamshire lying at your feet. Parts of this section are quite narrow and as there is good access it is suitable for wheelchairs, so take care and no speeding!

The trail crosses over Buttery Lane and swings right. At the time of writing there was a New Age site in the hollow on the right of the trail. Continue through another cycle gateway.

You have now rejoined the red Teversal route which you left at Longhedge Lane. Here there is a choice, to the right is Skegby (where there is accommodation) which has an old church rebuilt in 1870 due to mining subsidence, but the main route turns left onto the track. This return track to Pleasley runs parallel to the River Meden and at first runs high above the surrounding farmland before entering another deep cutting. A wild-flower book will come in particularly useful along this stretch and probably a butterfly book too.

The trail crosses Newbound Lane on a bridge then there is a steep, and loose surfaced drop down to Batley Lane. This is a tarmac lane watch out for vehicles as you cross before climbing up to the trail again. There is another short section in a cutting before the steep climb up to cross Longhedge Lane Bridle-path and down again to the track. Now the route is retracing the start of the ride and you continue until you have to turn left onto Pit Lane then right onto Chesterfield Road opposite the Pleasley Surgery. Cycle down the hill and turn left onto the footpath immediately after crossing the River Meden and just before the Post Office.

Turn left at the T-junction and follow the path through the woods, beside the river, back to the car park, taking care not to mow down any walkers or their dogs.

21. Pleasley Trails – Part 2

Distance: 3.75 miles

Route: Outgang Road Car Park – Common Lane – Pleasley Vale – Outgang Car Park.

Surface: Compacted soil and cinders, tarmac

Start: Outgang Road Car Park (SK509649)

Map: O.S. Landranger 120 & Pleasley Trails Network leaflet

Parking: Outgang Road Car Park

Accommodation: See previous ride

Comment: A short easy ride, ideal for an evening.

The Journey

From the car park cycle onto Outgang Road and turn right. The road runs parallel to the River Meden with the river on your right. It drops downhill through a well-wooded area to a sharp right-hand bend. On the left is a works entrance, so keep your ears open for approaching trucks. Round the bend are two delightful lodges. Beyond them, on the left is an old garden. Pass under some ancient yews and, a little further round the bend, you are faced with a colossal derelict mill astride the insignificant River Meden.

This is one of several large mills, all derelict, though one is being renovated for use as small industrial units. These are all that is left of the mighty Viyella firm. The oldest mill bears the date 1847. In 1970 there were 2000 workers. They spun yarn from wool shipped in from Australia and cotton from Sudan. The finished yarn was sent to Glasgow and returned as cloth to Nottinghamshire to be made into clothes.

The mills are an amazing sight in this small rural valley – and a sad one too. When the firm changed hands, the new owner allowed the business to run down before selling it to a foreigner who only really wanted the Viyella name. He closed the firm in the 1980s, thus bringing to an end one of our major industries. Unlike the pits, the mills died quietly, with very little national interest shown – a sore point among the local population.

The mills are on the right of the road which is gated from here – watch out for sleeping policemen too. On the left is a handsome stone house built at the turn of the century by one of the mill engineers. When he finished building it, the bosses were so horrified by the cost that they sacked him.

Beyond the mills a row of stone houses and a war memorial stand to the right of the road, which is on the boundary between Notts and Derbyshire. The road swings right and crosses the river. Another row of stone houses stands on the right and a little further along are some large buildings on the left, obviously unused. Opposite is a turning to a small car park, no sign again. Go through the car park and onto the old railway track.

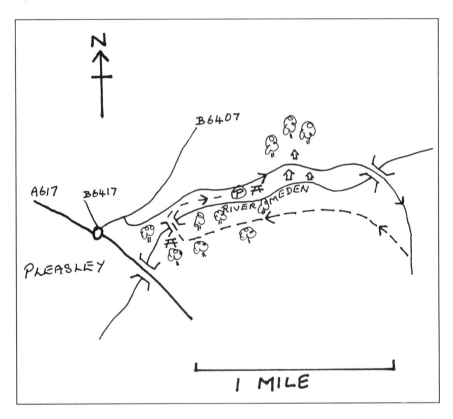

At first this passes through open farmland, then an area of red rock, then into thick trees. Take care if stopping in the rocky area there are several caves around. You may catch glimpses through the trees of the mills as you are passing along the ridge behind them. Follow the track as it drops down to the river valley. It joins the Meden Trail beside a picnic area. Turn right and follow the path to the bridge over the river. Cross the river and return to the car park.

Riding around Thrumpton

The following two rides are based at the tiny village of Thrumpton in the south west of the county close to the border with Leicestershire, one on-road, one off-road. On the route of the road ride, two gardens are occasionally open to the public: those of Thrumpton Hall (the Hall is open at the same times) and Sutton Bonington Hall. See The National Gardens Scheme leaflet for details. There is also a bridle-path which runs along the valley of the Trent from Thrumpton into the city of Nottingham which opens up this whole area of the county to those who prefer to use their cycles for transport. Several other rides in this book could be linked to give a pleasant week's riding (Bunny and the two Wysall rides, for instance). Following the valley of the River Soar south also leads into Leicestershire, another great cycling county full of surprises.

22. Thrumpton Road ride

Distance:	15 miles
Route:	Thrumpton — Kingston on Soar — Sutton Bonington — West Leake — East Leake — Gotham — Thrumpton
Surface:	Tarmac
Start:	Thrumpton (SK510310)
Map:	O.S. Landranger 129
Parking:	There is a small parking area opposite a row of old houses, near the telephone box.
Accommodation:	Manor Farm, Camping and Caravan Site, Thrumpton, Tel. 0115 983 0341; B&B at 5 Long Row, Kingston on Soar, Tel. 01509 673053.
Comment:	This is a pleasant village ride which threads an easy route through some hilly country, using river valleys. It is all on minor roads.

The Journey

Before setting off on the ride you should take at least a brief look at the village of Thrumpton. It is very small and will only take a few minutes. If you are camping turn right out of the campsite and follow the road as far as you can, about half a mile. On the way you will pass the only parking place, on the left, and opposite a terrace of interesting old estate houses. On your left is an entrance to the Hall and on the right, around the corner, is the 13th century church of All Saints. This has several graves of the Byron family in the church yard and a memorial in the church to Gervase Pigot, whose family owned Thrumpton for nearly 100 years in the 1600s. Beyond the church yard is Church House, dating from 1700, and extremely photogenic.

Thrumpton was known as Turmodestun when the Domesday Book was compiled in 1086, and the main land owners were Roger de Bully, William Peverel, and (a name we have not come across before) Hugh de Grandmesnil. The Hall was the home of the Putrell family for almost 600 years, until they were convicted of treason for hiding a conspirator involved in 'The Gunpowder Plot' of 1605 in a secret priest's hole built into a chimney breast. Since then the estate has been owned by a family who eventually became linked with the Byrons, by marriage; for twenty-eight years the vicar of Thrumpton was Lord Byron, who died in 1949.

If you are not able to be there on a day when the Hall and gardens are

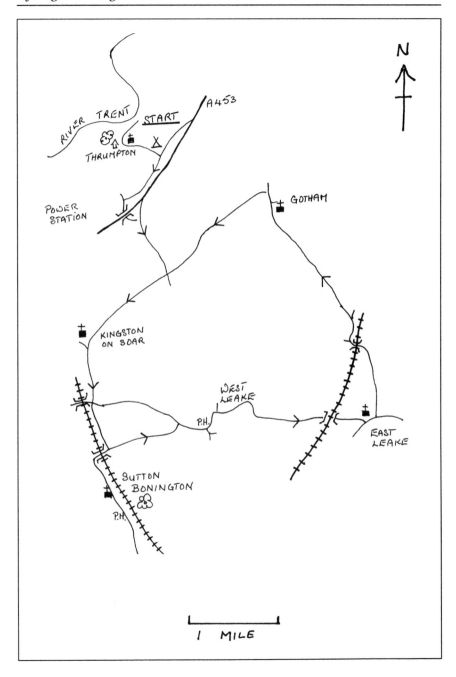

open to the public, the lovely brick entrance gateway to the Hall, just beyond Church House, and the estate houses may entice you back again. If you cycle past the Hall gateway and continue to the end of the road you will pass a depth pole on your left and a cottage called Ferry Side Cottage on your right before reaching a five-bar gate across the road. This is the start of the bridle route along the River Trent into Nottingham.

Now to begin the ride, retrace your tracks to the Manor Farm campsite then turn right at the T-junction. You have to reach the far side of the A453 which is the access road to Ratcliffe Power Station whose cooling towers can be seen over the hill behind Thrumpton as you approach from Nottingham. Luckily you can pass underneath the main road. The lane from Thrumpton climbs steeply until it is above the A453 then drops down to another T-junction, turn right, signposted to A453, Birmingham and West Leake. At the next T-junction turn left, following the same signposting, pass under the A453 and at the next T-junction turn right, signposted to West Leake.

Now you are zinging through open countryside, the power station is behind you, Winking Hill climbs steeply on your left and the land on the right drops down towards the River Soar. This section of the ride from the A453 to the crossroads you are approaching is the hilliest of the route but, unless you are really unfit, you will barely notice the undulations. At the crossroads turn right, signposted to Kingston.

The road passes Kingston Hall on your lef,. the home of Lord Belper, descendant of Jedediah Strutt who was born in Derbyshire (1726) and who worked with Arkwright to transform the manufacturing of cloth. Then, you reach a road junction. The route turns left here, signposted to Sutton Bonington, but first spare a moment or two to walk through the lychgate on your right and visit Kingston's church dedicated to St Winifred. The church is like a history book made of stone and we recommend purchasing the leaflet available which gives details of the two major families the Strutts (now Lord Belper), and the earlier Babingtons who came originally from Northumberland and built a church here in 1538. Inside the church is the most amazing monument to the Babingtons which includes 200 babes half hidden by barrels (tuns), Bab-in-tun!

Returning to the ride, take the lane to Sutton Bonington. Cross straight over the first crossroads and continue along College road with the University Campus (agricultural) buildings on your left. When the road bends right you turn left, signposted to West Leake, but for those interested in collecting yet another village, plus a garden, continue around the bend into Sutton Bonington before returning to this junction.

Continuing with the route, this lane is very narrow after passing the southern entrance to the Campus; passing places would be needed if there was any other traffic. At the T-junction turn right, signposted to West Leake again and in a quarter of a mile turn left just beyond The Star pub and again signed West Leake. The lane crosses the Kingston Brook which you crossed earlier after passing Kingston Hall. The lane bends sharp right and runs through the village of West Leake. There is a small Norman church, St Helen's, through the lychgate on the right and beyond footpaths lead across the fields to Kingston Brook with an ancient moated site close by.

St Wilfrid's church, Kingston on Soar

Through the village the road bends sharp right crosses the brook and then swings left to follow the line of the brook to East Leake. This is a much larger place, there is even a shop that sells cycles and spare parts! After passing the church of St Mary the Virgin, which has some Saxon herringbone masonry in one wall, turn left. There should be a pub on your right. Shortly turn left, signposted to Gotham and Leisure Centre. Continue along this road, with houses and a school on your right and open land on the left, as it swings sharp left, crosses a railway bridge, then swings sharp right. Continue ahead at the next junction, signposted to Gotham if the sign has been repaired. There is a golf course on your left which you will get to know a little better if you follow the Thrumpton Off-road ride.

This is not a particularly pleasant road compared to the lovely quiet lane you have been following, it is straight and traffic tends to travel rather fast, so take care. There is a bridle-path through the fields on the right but the route is not clear and a bit difficult to follow so it is probably best to stick to the road. Reaching Gotham you must pay a visit to the village church of St Lawrence. Some of it is 13th century and the tower and spire are quite unusual in that they were probably built at the same time. The stone spire is the only one in Nottinghamshire to be built to the same design as the earlier wooden spires. Inside the church used to be very colourful and hopefully English Heritage will restore the colours. There was a local family, called St Andrew, who lived at Rushcliffe Hall until the 17th century but Hall and family have disappeared, though there are memorials to them in the church.

Just beyond the church turn left, signposted to Kingston, and leave the village with the old school building, girls one end, boys the other, on your right. Continue to the crossroads, where you rejoin the outward route, and turn right. Cycle down the slope then up and around the edge of Winking Hill. Turn left before the A453, signposted to Nottingham, under the A453, right at the next junction, signposted to Nottingham again. Then turn left for Thrumpton and the end of the journey with a lovely last swoop down to the village.

23. Thrumpton Off-road ride

Distance: 11 miles

Route: Thrumpton – Gotham – East Leake – Thrumpton

Surface: Rough dirt bridle-paths, compacted farm tracks, tarmac.

Start: Thrumpton (SK510310)

Map: O.S. Landranger 129

Parking: Opposite terrace of old estate houses, near telephone box.

Accommodation: Manor Farm campsite, Thrumpton, Tel. 0115 983 0341. B&B Kingston on Soar, Tel. 01509 673053.

Comment: The entry for Thrumpton in The English Tourist Board's 'Domesday Book Then and Now', mentions an old trackway. Looking at a map of the area there is an obvious hilltop route from East Leake to Thrumpton and the old ferry crossing of the River Trent. This ride returns to Thrumpton from East Leake along this ancient route which is steeped in history and mythology. The going is often steep, both up and down, and sometimes very rough. If you are not used to off-road riding allow time for walking some bits. The views from these hills, circled by the previous low level road ride, are great. See the previous ride for details of the village of Thrumpton.

The Journey

Starting from Manor Farm campsite turn left out of their entrance, and immediately left again at the T-junction. Just beyond Manor Farm Yard entrance turn right onto a stony track, signposted 'Bridleway to Gotham', which climbs to a bridge over the A453. Over the bridge follow the bridleway signs to the right, running parallel to the A453 but with a tall, thick hedge between track and road. Follow the track when it turns left to cross a field, travelling away from the road, towards a cottage. Just beyond the cottage entrance is a gate; do not go through it but turn right and follow a narrow, overgrown, bridle-path with the cottage and its garden on your right. Take care along this path which is bumpy and stony, there is a ditch on the left hidden by the undergrowth.

The bridle-path becomes a sunken track with tall hawthorns forming an arch above. Go through the gate and bear left across the field towards Gotham Wood and beside the line of a sunken track.

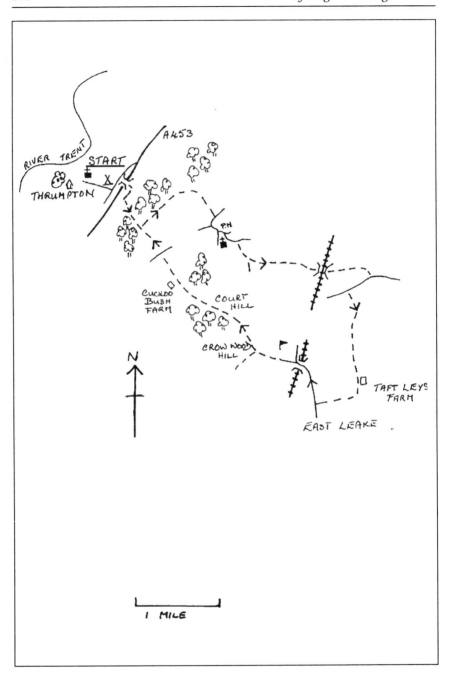

The track, which has been climbing steadily since passing the cottage, leads to a white gate into Gotham Wood (make sure you close the gate properly as you don't want to find the bull and his entourage breathing down your necks!). Here the track is really steep, muddy and rough as it wanders towards the top of the hill through this dark wood which reminded Bill that 'Batman lives in Gotham City'! Many walkers have trodden a path through the trees on the left of the track, it is narrow and there are tree roots but it is easier to walk along than to struggle through the mire left by the horses.

The path eventually leads to the top of Cottagers Hill and open country-side at the top of a wide track. Do not take this track but turn left, onto a signed bridleway, and follow the edge of Gotham Wood. You are about 90 metres above sea level with fantastic views across Gotham and Gotham Moor towards Bunny and Keyworth (two other rides). The path runs along the top of Gotham Hill with the wood and then a fence on your left, through another gate. Through this gate the safest route is to turn right, pick up the head of a sunken track and continue left across and down the field to a gate towards the bottom. Through the gate turn right into a wide track which takes you down to a tarmac road, bear right onto the road into Gotham village. It is thought that the name of Gotham comes from the Saxon for Goat, and Ham meaning home. Looking back up the steep hillside behind us it is easy to imagine it clothed in scrub and a perfect place for goats.

Continue along this road to the church passing a grocer's shop on your left and a pub with an unusual name, The Cuckoo Bush, on the right. The church of St Lawrence is well worth a visit before continuing with the ride.

Just before the church turn left, with The Sun pub on your left, then immediately right into Moor Lane. This lane bends sharp left and passes a row of substantial council houses. As you reach the last of these houses turn right onto a good wide vehicle track. Keep left when bridleways fork and at the next junction of tracks turn right, signposted 'Bridleway and Scatter-good'. Cross over old railway sleepers and follow the track as it bends left then turn left onto another signed bridle-path with the hedge on your left. Follow the path around the edge of the field to a footbridge. Cross this and bear left again, still keeping the hedge on your left. When you reach the corner of the field turn left again, there is a blue arrow here, through a gap in the hedge, then turn right and pass under the railway.

The route now follows wider tracks of varying quality, just as you think the surface is improving it deteriorates again. From the railway bridge there is a poor dirt track which joins a good track, keep straight on here. When this track turns sharp left you turn right onto another poor grass track, blue arrows again. This path takes you out to a tarmac road. Turn right onto the road. After passing Welldale Farm on your right turn left onto a signed bridleway. This is obviously an old road with hedges on both sides. It very quickly begins to climb a steep hill and vehicles have worn deep ruts in the dirt surface, watch out for pedal-high humps.

Almost at the top, near the Electricity pylons, there are plenty of places to stop for a rest and view the surroundings, the smoke appearing over the hill comes from the Gypsum works in East Leake. After the old track joins another from Hill Top Farm it drops steeply downhill, passing Taft Leys Farm, then bends right and takes you out past houses and school to a T-junction. Turn right here. There is a service road to the houses on your right you could use if the road is busy.

The road bends sharp left in front of the entrance to the Gypsum Works, crosses the railway, then swings right. At this point, keep straight on to a road with a sign for Rushcliffe Golf Club. The tarmac ends when you reach the entrance to the Golf Course and continue straight on onto a track of compressed red sand and stone. This track passes a house then shortly bends left. Here, turn right onto a grass, signed, bridle-path that runs along the top of the golf course across Crow Wood Hill. On the hillside below, unseen by us, are the remains of a moat; perhaps this is the site of the home of the St Andrews family, Rushcliffe Hall. A bit of the history of this area is included in the previous ride.

The path improves as it runs along the edge of the golf course with magnificent views across Gotham Moor to the right and forward to the earlier part of the route across Gotham Hill. Follow this path as it winds along the top of the hill, through a small copse and then continues straight ahead across a field with the hedge on your left. This is Court Hill. Go through the gate on the left in the corner of the field and turn right onto a rough track with a wood on your right. In the corner of this wood is a burial mound, again unseen by us, ahead is Cuckoo Bush Farm, and when you reach the farm the track to the left would take you to Crownend Wood.

Crownend Wood is reputed to be the place where the Saxons and Danes gathered, in the open air, to discuss and debate the local legal and administrative affairs of the thirty villages that made up the 'Hundred' (or shire) of Rushcliffe. The place was called a Moot.

Continue straight ahead passing Cuckoo Bush Farm on your left. It was here that we decided to stop and ask about the stories behind the strange name of the farm. David, the owner of the farm, was trying to repair an

The bridlepath along Gotham Hill – no sign of Batman!

ancient combine harvester (at least 25 years old) in the farm yard with his old dog Peg generally getting in the way. Bill crawled under the machine with him. They discussed the problem and began to fix it while David told us about Gotham and the surrounding area.

In the 12th century King John decided to build a hunting lodge in the area. We know from the stories of Robin Hood that much of the forest was strictly controlled by Forest Rangers. Perhaps the people of the Hundred of Rush-cliffe had been left to their own devices until then and no doubt the local population could see their days of hunting for the pot coming to an end. They decided to make it appear that the whole population of the area was mad and hoped this would make the King change his mind. At Cuckoo Bush Farm the villagers of Gotham planted a tall hedge around a cuckoo and when it flew away they lamented that they had not made it tall enough. Others stood a pig on a wall to watch a fair, or tried to drown an eel in a pond, or sent cheeses rolling downhill to Nottingham on their own.

Whether all these tactics worked, we cannot tell, but there is reputed to have been a castle in the area so they probably didn't. However, David's story-telling definitely worked as between them he and Bill fixed the old machine. Then he told us his last story.

He runs the farm single handed and a friend who had been helping with a two-man job said, 'What do you do when I'm not here to help you David?' 'The Good Lord provides!' was the answer. Give him a wave as you cycle by.

Follow the farm track as it runs steeply downhill. Cross straight over the tarmac road in the bottom and begin the even steeper climb up the far side of the valley. At the top you will find yourself at the top of Gotham Wood and you will begin to retrace the earlier part of the route as it runs through the wood, down the hill past the cottage and back into Thrumpton and the end of the ride.

24. East Markham

Distance:	11 miles
Route:	Milton – Bevercotes – East Markham – West Markham – Milton
Surface:	Tarmac and one long 'White Road', which is mostly excellent hard track.
Start:	Milton (SK716736)
Map:	O.S. Landranger 120
Parking:	The route starts at the Longbow Caravan Park, just off the A1; for those not camping there is a large commercial Truck Stop with catering facilities, opposite the Caravan Park.
Accommodation:	Longbow Caravan Park, Tel. 01777 838067. This is a small but very good touring site close to the A1. It may become very busy. There are also B&B facilities in Milton, for information contact: Retford Tourist Office, Tel. 01777 860780
Comment:	This is a very pleasant evening ride with good hostelries in East Markham, about two-thirds of the way round, the rest of the route is mostly downhill. There are several short sharp climbs which you may wish to walk. The route is mostly on minor roads and lanes, with about two miles of 'White Road'. Some minor lanes are exceedingly narrow, so listen for approaching traffic. There is at least one garden open to the public occasionally, in East Markham, and two unusual churches. For those interested in motor bikes there is a good Moto-Cross Track along the route.

The Journey

From the Longbow Caravan Site turn left onto the road. To the right is the roundabout junction of the A57, the A638 and the A1. Opposite the campsite is a very popular Truck Stop with trucks pulling out onto this minor lane all day! The route takes us through the village of Milton with an interesting butcher's on the left. There are donkeys and chickens in the paddock and a play area for children. On the right a little further on along the road is the entrance, through a farmyard, to a traditional cricket pitch with small green and white pavilion and fencing.

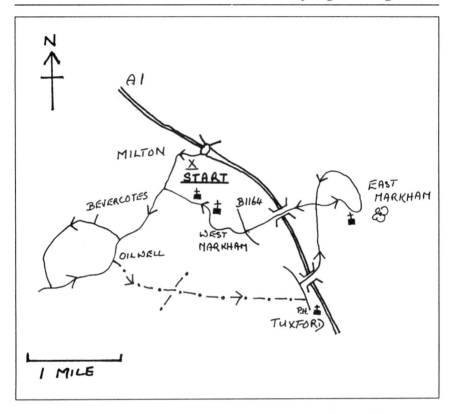

The lane continues through the village with houses on either side, passes a Water Authority Property on your left, and out into open farmland. When this lane makes a sharp left bend, turn right into a smaller lane, signposted to Bevercotes and with the Tourist Board's flower symbol sign. This symbol refers to the Mining Museum at Lound Hall, but with the closing of most of Nottinghamshire's coal mines this museum no longer exists, which seems odd to us, surely now is the time for the museum to be open. The first property along this lane is an Equestrian Centre, continue between tall hedges and farmyards, alive with cockerels and snorting pigs. This lane is exceptionally narrow and it is necessary to climb onto the steeply banked verge if anything else comes along.

Normally this is a very quiet lane, which skirts the foot of a steep hill. There is a Moto-Cross track on the hillside and on weekends the road could be busy.

Turn left at the T-junction and continue along this road, past a track on the right to a large white house, and another to Farleys Wood. Take the next track on the right just before a small oil well with two nodding donkey engines. The track is an old country road. It may have been created at the time the local parish was enclosed, possibly early 19th century, as it is a very straight track, only kinking as it climbs the hill. Most really old roads bend and twist far more.

Though no longer used as a road, the track is used by farm vehicles and may be deeply rutted. Once up the main part of the hill the track undulates between hedges with open farmland on either side, where it crosses a small stream the going may be a bit boggy in places. Continue until reaching another track, the junction is virtually a T-junction. Your route, which is the most used track, turns right, then bears left at the next junction. You now have a long, straight, gentle run down towards Tuxford. The 14th century tower and spire of the church of St Nicholas, visible slightly to the right, stands over this ancient market town which was first granted a Charter to hold a weekly market by King Henry III in 1218.

When the track reaches the B1164 on the edge of Tuxford, the town centre lies to the right but you turn left onto a 'B' road and immediately begin to climb a hill. Take the first right, signposted to East Markham, which climbs even more steeply to bridge the roaring traffic of the A1. Luckily this major road is in a slight cutting and the sound of traffic quickly dies away as you continue into open countryside. When a crossroads is reached, turn right to make a tour of East Markham, part of Roger de Bully's land at the time of the Domesday Book.

This is a large village nestling in a triangle of land between the A57, the A1, and the railway line from Newark to Retford and the north. There is a handsome church with some extraordinary gargoyles, monuments to the two famous Markham judges of the 14th century (father and son), and to Elizabeth Cartwright (pen-name Mrs Markham), who wrote a history of England in 1823 and a history of France in 1828. There are some interesting old houses in the village, several shops and Inns, and to the north and west are orchards.

From the crossroads at the top of the village where you turned right, cycle downhill, then begin to climb. On the right is a white wooden fence and here you turn right into Church Street. The road bends left in front of the church of St John the Baptist. Turn left into Plantation Road. Soon you will pass The Queens Head and a shop. Continue to a War Memorial on your left and a crossroads with The Rose and Crown on the corner. To the right there is a farm shop that sells local produce, well worth a visit with supper in mind.

A privately-restored windmill at Tuxford

the route turns left at this crossroads and shortly begins quite a steep climb up Beckland Hill.

This brings you back to the crossroads where you entered the village. Turn right, and watch for the orchards on your right. Again, cross the A1, pass a windmill on your left and continue to the B1164. Cross straight over and go down a steep hill into West Markham.

Cycling into West Markham is a little like cycling through a time warp. To begin with you won't find any reference to West Markham if you are looking for historical notes. There is no mention of it in Nottinghamshire's *A Visitor's Guide to Churches in Nottinghamshire*. Even Arthur Mee, whose guides to The King's England ran into 38 volumes and who was born and lived in Nottinghamshire, does not mention it. Yet there is an entry in 'The Domesday Book, England's Heritage, Then and Now,' (1985) but under the heading Markham Clinton. The entry reads 'Westmarcham: Roger de Bully from Claron and 6 Frenchmen from him'. Another look at Arthur Mee reveals that he too calls this tiny community Markham Clinton.

Another reason for feeling out of step with time here is that if you are of pre-war vintage (and a very good vintage it is too!) it reminds one of villages back in the 1940s and 1950s. There is no shop or pub, just a cluster of houses and farms around a west facing open triangular field. On reaching the first houses of the village bear left and follow the lane around this central triangle, turning right at the bottom. Look up the field, has this always been an open green or are all those ridges and platforms in the field the site of the original village? And was its name Markham Clinton or West or Little Markham?

The village has a good feel about it but the real treat is to come. On the next corner of the village triangle, the route turns left. On this corner is a particularly unusual old church. Most churches are substantial and often beautiful, they make a statement about the state of religion and the wealth of the local community at different periods of their existence, and they are so obviously intended for religious worship. Originally, the church was also the village meeting place, the place where the community decided all their local affairs, even a place where the wake for a local farmer was held and large quantities of ale and cheese consumed. Can you imagine a funeral 'party' of this nature in most of our churches today?

The church of All Saints, 'Westmarcham' in the Domesday Book, looks far more part of the local community than any beautiful great stone edifice. It has timbered gables and a timber tower, there is flint-like Saxon masonry, a Norman priest's door, and until the restoration of 1949 there were mud floors inside. There is something warm and welcoming about this little building which was abandoned in the 1830s, when the nearby Mausoleum was built which you see later on the ride, until the villagers demanded its restoration as the village church.

When you can tear yourself away from this lovely peaceful spot continue along the tree-lined lane to the left of the church. On your right you will see another amazing sight, for standing among the trees is a classical temple with an impressive portico on the east end and a tower topped by a cupola in the centre of the now-derelict building. This is the Mausoleum built to replace the homely church you have just visited. It contains a monument to the Duchess of Newcastle, Georgiana, who died giving birth to twins.

Continue down the steep hill and turn right at the T-junction at the bottom. Now the route retraces the early part of the journey through Milton to the Caravan Park and the end of the ride. If you look back as you cycle through the village you can see the cupola of the Mausoleum above the trees.

25. Bothamsall Off-road

Distance: 13.5 miles

Route: Milton – Bevercotes – Bothamsall – Walesby – West Markham – Milton

Surface: Tarmac; just about every conceivable type of bridlepath/farm track surface imaginable, from sand to cinder.

Start: Milton (SK716736)

Map: O.S. Landranger 120

Parking: For those not camping there are several eating places on the A1 roundabout, including the Truck Stop.

Accommodation: Longbow Caravan Park, Milton Road, Milton, Newark, Notts. Tel. 01777 860780. This site is small, friendly, and has excellent facilities. There is also B&B available in Milton, for details contact Retford Tourist Office, Tel. 01777 860780.

Comment: This ride offers many distractions travelling as it does in a circle from the busy A1. It passes a cricket ground, ancient fortifications, Robin Hood's cave, a shimmering silver birch forest, and The World of Robin Hood. Looping around the valley of the Rivers Meden and Maun it is virtually free of hills, and in dry weather not a difficult off-road ride. A good family ride.

The Journey

The ride begins at the Longbow Caravan Park, Milton, turn left onto the road towards Milton village. Take care here as there are usually several heavy trucks either leaving the Truck Stop opposite, or approaching from the A1. The road makes a sharp left bend before entering the village and once the houses are reached watch for a signed bridle-path on the right which drops down between the houses to a bridge over the River Maun. Take this bridle-path, cross the bridge, pass through a gate (remember to close it), and cross the field beyond.

On your left is one of the loveliest cricket grounds we have found in Nottinghamshire. The entrance to the ground is through a farm yard in the village. The bridle-path reaches a gate and a ditch, then should continue straight on but there is now a fenced path to the left and right, perhaps the spoil tip ahead has created the need for a change in direction. Turn left onto

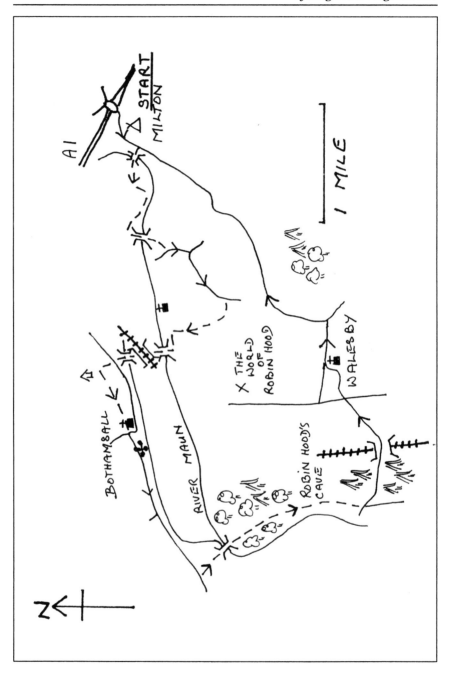

this path which will take you to the bank of the River Maun, where it turns right and follows the river to Lound Hall. Herons and ducks are your companions here. Follow the river and turn left onto the track which crosses the river and wends a way through the buildings of Lound Hall. This once was a Training and Conference Centre and mining museum. When you reach the road, turn left. To the right is Bevercotes Colliery which was the first push-button colliery in the world and opened in 1967.

Continuing with the ride, you have turned left out of the Lound Hall grounds, cycle out to Bevercotes, two farms and an equestrian centre, and turn right at the T-junction. This lane rises slightly as it skirts around a small hill. It is also extremely narrow with steep banks, listen for approaching traffic. Fortunately this is normally a very quiet lane but around the corner you will see a well laid out moto-cross track, perhaps one of the best grounds for spectators around, and if there is a meeting this lane could be busy. Turn right opposite the moto-cross site onto a wide track between hedges. Follow this track, which swings sharp right shortly, to a T-junction of tracks. Turn left here. The remains of the Chapel of St James are along the track to the right, among a group of trees, but there is no way of getting to it at present. It was the chapel to a great house, the home of the Holles family, in the 16th to 18th centuries including Denzil Holles who was Lord Mayor of London in 1599, before the different branches of the family lived at Welbeck and Clumber.

Turn right and cross the bridge over the river Maun and continue to the road, with Haughton Hall Farm on your left. Look for the unusual top to one of the farm buildings. The track passes under a railway bridge before reaching the B6387, which you cross straight over and continue up the drive to a handsome house called Haughton Park House. Turn left in front of the house (do you think the veranda in the roof is anything to do with that strange top to the farm building down at Haughton Hall Farm?) and follow the gated track into Bothamsall. This track is part of the Robin Hood Way.

Bothamsall is a very attractive village which frequently wins The Best Kept Village competition. The church, on your left, was rebuilt in the mid-19th century by the Duke of Newcastle. Cross straight over, on reaching a proper road, signposted to Thoresby and Warsop. The road climbs a slight rise to Castle Hill where, on your left, the earthworks of a Norman motte and bailey castle are now crowned with a good thatch of trees. It is easy to see why this spot was chosen as a site for a castle: this is on the northern edge of Sherwood Forest with the valley of the Maun and Meden below.

Continue along the road passing a turning on the right and taking the bridle-path on the left before reaching the A614. This is part of the Robin Hood Way and signed Bridle Road to Walesby & Ollerton. This is the start of a really splendid off-road section of the ride, the route runs down the edge of the field with the hedge on your right and enters the wood ahead after crossing a small wooden bridge over the River Maun. Turn right onto the forest path over the bridge which winds a way through Blackcliffe Plantation. There is an up hill section which may need to be walked but then you are out onto open heathland where you bear right, keeping the shimmering silver birch trees on your right.

This path, known as Kings Ride, is soft sand in places. Soon you will find you are cycling above a small stream which meanders along below the bank on your right, this is called Whitewater. There is an outcrop of rocks between the path and river and here you will find Robin Hood's Cave. The path now has trees on the left and shortly you reach the road. This is the end of the off-road riding, the return to camp is by road. Turn left onto this lane and continue through the trees, passing the International Scout campsite on your left, cross over a railway bridge and then straight over the B6387 into Main Street Walesby.

The village butcher's, Milton

Here there is a short but worthwhile diversion. Instead of crossing straight over the B6387, turn left and cycle out of Walesby to visit The World of Robin Hood where you will find replicas of medieval villages and siege machines, etc.

Returning to the crossroads, turn left into the village of Walesby where there are a couple of shops and two Inns, The Carpenters Arms and The Red Lion (which has a notice 'No Cycling in the Car Park!). Turn right into Tuxford Road with the church of St Edmund on the right. Continue to a T-junction under Hanging Hill Plantation where you turn left. Keep straight on, passing the turning to Bevercotes on the left, through Milton, noting the entrance to the cricket ground on the left in the village, and return to the start at the Caravan Park.

26. Colston Bassett On-road ride

Distance: 19 miles

Route: Stragglethorpe – Cotgrave – Owthorpe – Colston Bassett – Cropwell Bishop – Cropwell Butler – Radcliffe on Trent – Stragglethorpe.

Surface: Tarmac

Start: Thornton's Holt campsite (SK639376)

Map: O.S. Landranger 129

Parking: Close to Thornton's Holt campsite is Shepherd's Inn, a good place to start and end the ride if not camping. Remember to ask permission.

Accommodation: Thornton's Holt campsite, Stragglethorpe, Radcliffe on Trent, Nottingham, NG12 2JZ. Tel. 0115 933 2125. This is a very clean, pleasant site and though it is beside a railway, this only serves the Stragglethorpe Mine and does not seem to disturb the peace at all. For other details contact Nottingham Tourist Office, Tel. 0115 947 0661.

Comment: This is a hilly ride, with one very steep hill, but all on minor roads and small lanes. There is a bird sanctuary at Radcliffe on Trent and private gardens open to the public during the summer – see The National Gardens Scheme, for which a leaflet is available from any Tourist office. The route also passes Holme Pierrepont, the National Water Sports Centre, for details of events contact the Centre on Tel. 0115 982 1212.

The Journey

Turn left out of the campsite and follow the road as it climbs past Stragglethorpe Nurseries and around Stragglethorpe Mine. Take the first turning on the right, opposite Hollygate Farm and signposted to Cotgrave and Plumtree. Continue straight on in Cotgrave on Bingham Road. Turn left in the village centre, into Scrimshire Lane, signposted to Owthorpe, with the church on your right. This becomes Owthorpe Road and is the start of a really steep hill, Wolds Hill, warranting an arrow on the O.S. map. Cross straight over the A46 and take care as you drop down Owthorpe Hill which is equally steep.

At the crossroads, go straight on but turn left briefly and visit the hamlet

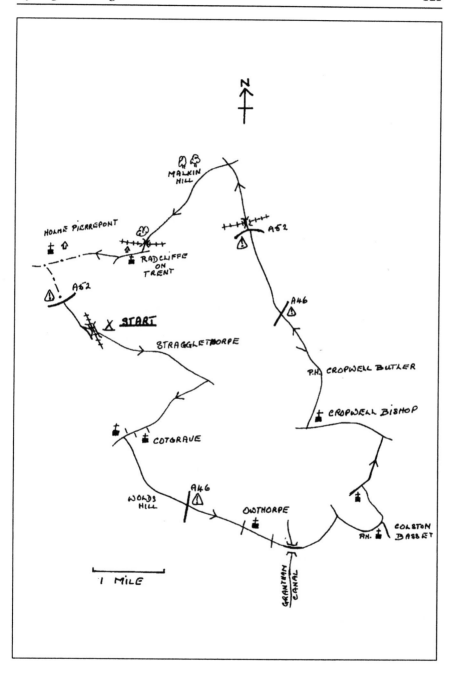

of Owthorpe where the tiny remains of the old church (1705) stand in a field behind a farm. Straight over the next crossroads, signposted to Colston Bassett. The road crosses the Grantham Canal before reaching a T-junction at Sand-pit Hollow. Turn right into Hall Lane. The Hall and all its magnificent buildings are on your left as you cycle along the tree-lined road into Colston Bassett. After passing the church, on your right, the road bends sharp right, keep straight on signposted to Tithby and Bingham. The lane crosses the River Smite before climbing the hill past the cricket ground to a T-junction.

Turn right, signposted to Cropwell Bishop, but do spare a few moments to visit the ruins of the old church overlooking the cricket ground to the left.

Returning to the route turn left at the T-junction and continue into Cropwell Bishop. Turn right beside the church for Cropwell Butler where the road bends sharp left then sharp right. The sign in the village indicates a crossroads ahead but it seems more like a forked junction. Take the right fork, Hardy Gate Road, and continue to the A46. Cross straight over and continue to the A52. This junction is less easy as you have to turn left onto the A52 then immediately right, signposted to Shellford. The road crosses a railway bridge then, narrow and unfenced, crosses open fields before dropping down to a crossroads. Here, turn left and run along the face of the Malkin Hills towards Radcliffe on Trent. Be thankful that it is not 1487 or you may have to stand aside and wait as King Henry VII and his army march along the hills to defeat the Earl of Lincoln, the pretender to the throne Lambert Simnel, and their army which included 2000 German mercenaries at the battle of East Stoke.

All is now peaceful and you can enjoy the view across the Trent Valley just as King Henry did over 500 years ago. Radcliffe on Trent, called Radclyve in the Domesday Book, is a surprisingly handsome town with many old red brick houses. It stands on a 100-foot wooded cliff above the river where yachts bob gently at their moorings.

The road into Radcliffe passes over a railway then at the crossroads turn right, signposted to Nottingham, and continue straight on through the congested shopping street passing the church on your left and a pub on your right. Turn right, opposite the bus depot, into The Green. This becomes a gated private road with sleeping policemen.

On your right is Holme Pierrepont Hall and a short diversion along the lane to the right will take you to the tiny village of the same name. The church, St Edmund's, was first mentioned in 1201 but almost completely rebuilt about 1666 though it contains several interesting old monuments including a brass from about 1383. Holme Pierrepont Hall is a handsome early Tudor brick manor house with a secret courtyard garden. The Hall, which is still privately owned, is open to the public on a limited number of days a week from June onwards. Tel. 0115 933 2371 for details.

Returning to the route from the village, continue straight on with Holme Pierrepont Hall on your right and, probably, a flock of Jacob sheep in the field, too. Opposite the entrance to the Hall turn left along the 'No Through Road' to The Gables. Continue past the house to the A52. It is possible to cross safely here but as the track you have just used is no longer a road, none of the traffic lights face us, so great care is needed.

The route crosses straight over the A52 and continues, taking the left fork at the next junction but noting the pub on the right fork, to the Thornton's Holt campsite.

27. Colston Bassett Off-Road ride

Distance: 15 miles

Route: Stragglethorpe – Cotgrave – Clipston – Owthorpe –
                     Colston Bassett – Cropwell Bishop – Cropwell Butler –
                     Stragglethorpe.

Surface: Minor roads; Tracks; Bridle Trails (many very muddy and
                     cut-up by horses after rain).

Start: Thornton's Holt campsite (SK639376)

Map: O.S. Landranger 129

Accommodation: Thornton's Holt campsite, Stragglethorpe, Tel. 0115 933
                     2125

Comment: This is an off-road ride through beautiful countryside with
                     steep hills both up and down. It is not a beginner's ride
                     and is only recommended for dry weather. The route
                     complements the on-road Colston Bassett ride.

The Journey

Turn right out of the campsite, under the railway bridge and immediately left. On your right is the long, low, thatched Shepherd's Inn. This road crosses the disused Grantham Canal which has water in it at this point, and when reaching Cotgrave, turn right into Plumtree Road, with one of Cotgrave's churches on your right. This road leads out of the village. It is gently undulating. Take the first turning left, signposted to Clipston, up a very steep climb through a stand of trees. When the lane bends sharp right a track goes left through the trees towards open fields. This is a RUPP – a Road Used as Public Path. Bridle Trails in Nottinghamshire are clearly marked with a fat blue arrow, usually on a short dumpy post, so look down for signs rather than up.

The track, which is well-used both by cyclists and horses, goes straight ahead with the hedge on your right, then turns sharp right. There is a steady climb from about 60 metres to over 90 metres at the top of Wolds Hill where another track crosses your route. Continue straight on to the A46. Cross this busy road with great care. The RUPP continues through Borders Wood, the first hundred yards or so is newly laid quarry waste – and this may well be extended. Continue straight ahead down the steep hill through the wood and across the fields to the road.

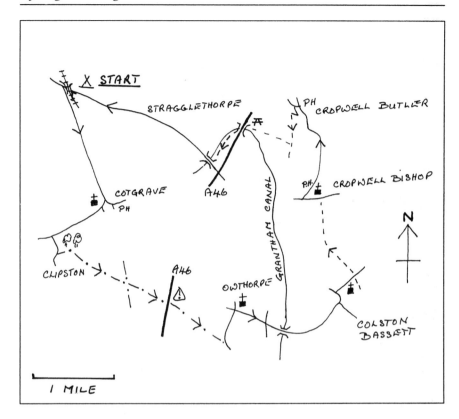

Turn left onto the road and continue to Owthorpe crossroads. At the crossroads turn right.

Diversion:

If you wish to make a brief diversion to Owthorpe, go straight over at the crossroads. Owthorpe reminds one of a battlefield with the road full of bomb craters and muck, though there are a few lovely buildings here. A grass lane leads to the church of St Margaret which dates from 1705 and hides behind a farmyard on your right. The church has a double-decker Jacobean pulpit and a screen which was originally in Owthorpe Hall, demolished in the 19th century.

Main Route:

Straight over the next crossroads, over the Grantham Canal and at the

A gargoyle on the ruined tower of St Mary's church, Colstan Bassett

T-junction, at Sand-pit Hollow on the outskirts of Colston Bassett, turn left and take the first right. This lane crosses a stream then climbs the hill. On your right are the ruins of a lovely old church, St Mary's, which is reputed to have been one of the most beautiful in the County and well worth a short visit.

Continue along the lane to Home Farm where, opposite the track to the church, there is a bridle-path sign. The bridle-path continues straight on when the farm track swings right into the farmyard. The path is signed, it can also be wet. It crosses the top of the first field against the farmhouse garden hedge, crosses a track from the farm and continues through the gate ahead. If you are really hoping to get muddy now is your chance this is the worst gateway we've experienced for years! After passing under the electricity cables the path joins a track, which is a great improvement, down to the road into Cropwell Bishop.

Turn left onto the road into Cropwell Bishop and right after the church, signposted to Cropwell Butler. There are shops and a pub in Cropwell Bishop. In Cropwell Butler, stay on the main road through this pretty village until the road forks. Take the left fork and immediately left again into Back Lane and shortly right into Hoe Lane. Though these lanes are one-way they are so narrow there is barely room for a modern car, so keep your ears open for approaching traffic and watch out for escape routes.

Hoe Lane becomes a pleasant bumpy, dirt track as it leaves the village behind. There is even a new wooden seat if you are feeling weary. Continue past the seat and down the hill towards the houses of Cropwell Bishop. Just around a right-hand bend there is a bridle-path on the right that will take you, possibly wetly, to the Grantham Canal Picnic Site on the A46. Don't be surprised to find the canal is short of a vital component, water!

To finish the ride, cross the bridge over the canal, just before the picnic site, to the tow-path on the left bank of the canal. Follow the tow-path under the A46 and continue to a minor road. Turn right onto the road and follow down to Thornton's Holt campsite.

28. Flintham

Distance: 12 miles or 13 miles if off-road routes followed.

Route: Hawksworth – Thoroton – Sibthorpe – Elston – Flintham
                 – Screveton – Hawksworth

Surface: Tarmac

Start: Hawksworth (SK434753)

Map: O.S. Landranger 129

Parking: This village has excellent, wide grass verges on the
                 approach roads which are obviously used by those going
                 hunting in the area for parking horseboxes, etc.

Comment: Both these rides are easy-going along quiet country
                 lanes with wide views on all sides, yet there is sufficient
                 rise and fall to make the ride interesting. There are private
                 gardens occasionally open to the public at Elston,
                 Screveton, and Flintham, see The National Gardens
                 Scheme leaflet for details. On a clear day it is possible
                 to see Belvoir Castle to the south east across the Vale
                 of Belvoir. The bridle-paths in the area are heavily used
                 by horses and the couple of off-road optional extras are
                 not suitable for the novice.

The Journey

From the church of St Mary and All Saints, in the centre of Hawksworth,
cycle south and turn left for Thoroton at a weirdly off-set crossroads (perhaps someone on the council was saving costs on sign boards) and at the
T-junction turn left again, signposted to Shelton. There is a gentle climb to
another crossroads where you turn left, drop down to cross Back Dyke and
climb again to another crossroads. Here, turn right and cross open farmland
(no fences or hedges to shelter you from the wind) towards a cluster of
houses well-sheltered by tall Leylandii hedges called Top Green on the O.S.
map but with a signboard that announces Sibthorpe.

As you emerge from the sheltering conifers, Sibthorpe's 60ft tall dovecote
is on your right. This 14th century dovecote has 1260 nesting places in 28
tiers and is now owned by the National Trust. The most dominating sight is
that of the twenty Irish yew trees in the churchyard ahead, reputed to be
1000 years old. Most of the churchyards in this area have beautiful yews from
which bows and arrows were said to be made, but these trees in St Peter's

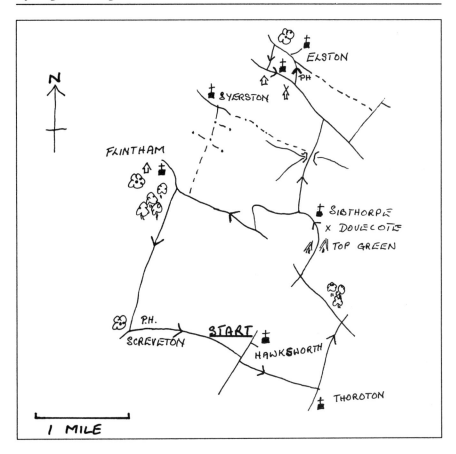

churchyard are the most magnificent. The tower of St Peter's is 14th century and the stones in its base are weathered into amazing shapes.

The route continues past the church and through the village which is hardly more than a farm yard with all its old barns converted into housing. On the far side of the village bear right on a bend in front of a cottage and signposted to Elston. This lane leads across open farmland again to a T-junction. Here the main, on-road, route turns left for Elston.

Off-road Alternative:

Turn right at T-junction and take first left just after crossing a narrow dyke. In about half a mile there is an unmarked bridle-path on your left which has a hedge on the right and crosses a field to a stand of willows. If you reach a farm track on your right to Devon Farm you have gone too far. This bridle-path is muddy. It bridges a dyke and continues across the fields to Elston.

Main Route:

From the T-junction the road runs straight into the village of Elston with a converted windmill, minus sails and cap, on your left. Turn right into Toad Lane, The Chequers is on your right. You circle the village before heading back towards Sibthorpe. Continue past The Chequers to a T-junction, those who took the off-road option will enter the village from the right, the main route turns left. Just around the bend is a small lane on the right which will take you to visit an old, unused chapel with a zigzag decorated Norman doorway.

Return to the route that circles the village and turn left again just as it runs out into open countryside. The lovely gardens of the village are on your left. At the next T-junction turn left again. On your right is the long grey Hall where William Darwin of Lincolnshire came to live after his marriage to the heiress of the Waring family. William was the Great, Great, Grandfather of Charles Darwin who was to set the world into uproar with his revolutionary ideas on evolution.

Long before Charles appeared on the scene, William's off-spring were developing the enquiring minds that must have given him so much encouragement. Robert, William's son, developed a love of science, his son Robert wrote *Principia Botanica* and his son Erasmus was a poet and scientist who invented many domestic and industrial machines. The 13th century church is on your left and contains many memorials to the Darwin family and opposite is a row of almshouses built by Ann Darwin.

Continue straight on and, when you reach Toad Lane on your left, you will know that you have circled the village. Keep straight on, passing the windmill on your right and turn right at the first junction, signposted to Sibthorpe. Here there is another difficult off-road option.

Off-road Option:

In less than half a mile, as the lane passes under electricity cables and over a stream, there is a bridle-path on the right which will take you into the tiny, isolated village of Syerston. On reaching the village take the first lane on the left, this soon becomes a track which runs south. On reaching a crossroads of tracks take the bridle-path straight ahead which will take you into Flintham.

Main Route:

Take the first right on the outskirts of Sibthorpe, signposted to Flintham, and turn right again at the T-junction, again for Flintham. As you enter Flintham the off-roaders rejoin the main route from the right and on the left is an old Pinfold. The village is very pretty and was the home of the Hose family from the 13th century until the 17th century. To visit the church pass the public house on your right and as the road bends sharp right keep straight on to what appears to be a private lane. On your left is the tall wall of the Hall's walled garden with fruit trees peeping over the top, and a variegated holly hedge with a few taller hollies clipped like lollipops. The church is on the right just before the lane becomes a narrow snicket. If you keep straight on along this stone-paved snicket, you will come to the back wall of Flintham's unique conservatory with tall palms and climbers peeping through the high windows. Here there is also a gateway into the churchyard of St Augustine's which has a 13th century tower and some interesting herringbone stone-work and memorials to the Hose family including one Richard Hacker who is thought to have founded the church.

Leaving the churchyard return to the road and retrace your route through the village. Take the turning on the right signposted to Screveton, and cycle down the hill from the village. When you reach a lake on your right stop for a moment and look back up the hill through the trees and you will see Flintham Hall, built last century, standing at the top of the hill.

Continue to Screveton and turn left for Hawksworth, passing the Royal Oak on your left, and continue to the T-junction at Hawksworth. Turn left for the village centre.

29. Car Colston

Distance:	10 miles
Route:	Hawksworth – Screveton – Car Colston – Scarrington – Aslockton – Thoroton – Hawksworth
Surface:	Tarmac
Start:	Hawksworth (SK434753)
Map:	O.S. Landranger 129
Parking:	Hawksworth village is surrounded by lanes probably created in the early years of enclosure during the latter half of the 18th century, when each new, straight lane was bordered by a very wide grass verge, a ditch, and a hedge. These make excellent pull-offs and even after a long wet winter, most seem firm.
Comment:	This is an easy-going ride, all on minor roads, through several lovely old villages. Hawksworth is a very small village with Wars of the Roses connections. A footpath leads across one of the battlefields towards Thoroton from the end of Town Street, beside the church. Down this road there is also a small general store and a handsome Manor House.

The Journey

Cycle south west from the centre of Hawksworth and take the first turning on the right, signposted to Screveton. The land is flat around here and there are several dykes. There are horses in the fields to the left and shortly, on your right, is a stable that specializes in trotting. If you are lucky you may see one of these high-stepping beauties out training. Screveton is even smaller than Hawksworth, but it does have a pub, The Royal Oak (Home Ales), which may not be open during the day out of the summer season. At the first junction turn left, signposted to Car Colston, and continue for less than a quarter of a mile then turn left down the lane to St. Wilfrids, Screveton church. This church dates from the early 13th century and contains a memorial to Richard Whalley, who lived nearby, who had three wives and 25 children! Just outside the porch is a sun dial dated 1732, and beside the churchyard is a timber frame cottage with herringbone brickwork.

Returning to the road, continue towards Car Colston which used to be a gated village but now the gates have been removed – modern man cannot spare the time to open and close gates! That is a great shame as this is a lovely

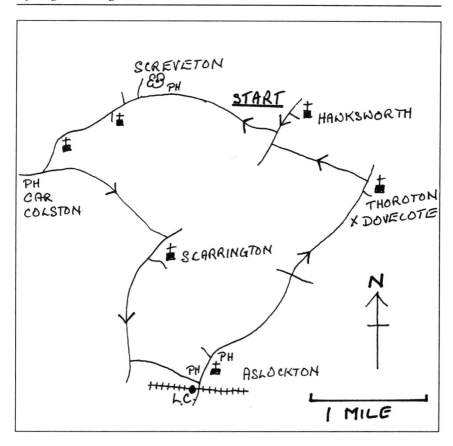

old village with the largest green in the county of Nottinghamshire. There is one green as you enter the village then another even larger on the other side of the village and as you stand at the T-junction on the green The Royal Oak stands on the far side to your right. Car Colston was the home of Dr Robert Thoroton, born 1623, who wrote Antiquities of Nottinghamshire.

The route turns left at the T-junction on the green and leaves the village heading for Scarrington. At the next T-junction turn right and cycle into the quiet village of Scarrington. Turn left by the church, with its 14th century tower topped by a spire, and almost immediately on your right is a tower of 50,000 used horseshoes standing 17ft high and reputed to weigh 17 tons, collected by a post-war blacksmith and now owned by the County Council. Behind the tower is a restored pinfold which is the place where straying animals were held until their owners paid a fine for their release. Return to the T-junction by the church and go straight over, signposted to Bingham and A52, a lane which leaves the village with Manor Farm on your right.

In about three quarters of a mile turn left, signposted to Aslockton, and continue to the T-junction in Aslockton. To the right is a level crossing and tiny railway station, but you turn left. On your left is The Old Greyhound, with Home Brewery and an excellent pub garden and children's play area, on the right is the post office and general store. A little further along the road is another pub and a general store, and the modern church is on your right.

Aslockton is the birthplace of Thomas Cranmer, the virtual creator of the Church of England, who suggested to Henry VIII that he should have his marriage to Catherine invalidated by English clergy. Behind the church is a path called Cranmer's Walk and an ancient moated mound known as Cranmer's Mound.

The tiny railway station at Aslockton

Continue straight out of the village, straight over the crossroads, towards Thoroton. Note how straight and wide the road is from hedge to hedge, obviously a road planned on a surveyor's drawing board when the parish was enclosed during the late 18th or early 19th century, when the large open fields shared by the community were divided, hedged and ditched.

On entering the village of Thoroton the first thing to note is the round 14th century thatched dovecote on your right. A little further on through this attractive village take the lane on the right to visit the 14th century church of St Helen with a tiny Saxon window. Thoroton typifies the villages in the area with houses and cottages built mostly of red brick. It is very easy to dismiss brickwork as all Victorian, especially if one lives in an industrial town or city. Take a close look at this brickwork and you may notice the uneven size of the bricks, also the variations in colour, quality, and methods of laying. Many of these houses were built long before Victoria's reign – Holme Pierrepont Hall is an early Tudor building. The use of bricks was originally a status symbol but, by 1700, they were often used to build chimneys on less pretentious houses and, later in the century, brick farmhouses became common. Most of the bricks will have been produced locally and made from local clay, which is why the colour of the houses blends so beautifully with the surrounding farmland. As a rough guide the smaller the brick the older it is. In 1571, the statutory size was nine by four-and-a-half, by two-and-a-quarter inches. In 1784 and 1850, brick taxes led to an increase in their size. Today, these old brick houses make beautiful backdrops to Nottinghamshire's lovely gardens.

Returning to the road, take the first left and right at the T-junction into Hawksworth.

30. Stanton on the Wolds

Distance: 12 miles
Route: Wysall — Willoughby in the Wolds — Widmerpool — Stanton on the Wolds — Keyworth — Wysall.
Surface: Tarmac
Start: Wysall (SK604273)
Map: O.S. Landranger 129
Accommodation: Brooklea Farm, Wysall, Tel. 01509 880792. This is a very small site with minimal facilities. For details of other accommodation in the area, Tel. 0115 977 4212 or 0115 947 0661.
Comment: Wysall is a small, pretty village on the edge of the Wolds; this is a hilly ride but all on minor roads. The route starts at the car park of The Plough, a lovely 'Old World' Inn which serves huge meals, at lunchtime, suitable for cyclists and has a roaring log fire that warms the cockles of your heart on cold blustery days. Do remember to ask the publican for permission to leave your vehicle in the car park while you are off cycling. There are gardens open to the public occasionally in both Stanton on the Wolds and Keyworth.

The Journey

From the Plough car park turn right onto the road and take the first left, signposted to Widmerpool, and then the first right, signposted to Willoughby. As with most roads in the Wolds the terrain is undulating, but not stressfully so. On your left along here is Glebe Lodge Stables and you can see from the state of the grass verges that there are many horses in the area. Take the first turning left into Willoughby on the Wolds, signposted to Upper Broughton.

A short diversion down a small lane on your left will take you to the church which holds many monuments to the Willoughby family who lived in the village from the 13th century and eventually owned Wollaton Hall, which now belongs to Nottingham County Council. Part of the family house can be seen in the farmhouse and cottage near the church. The last battle of the Civil War, in Nottinghamshire, took place near Willoughby and it is said that villagers climbed the church tower to watch as the Royalists, under Sir

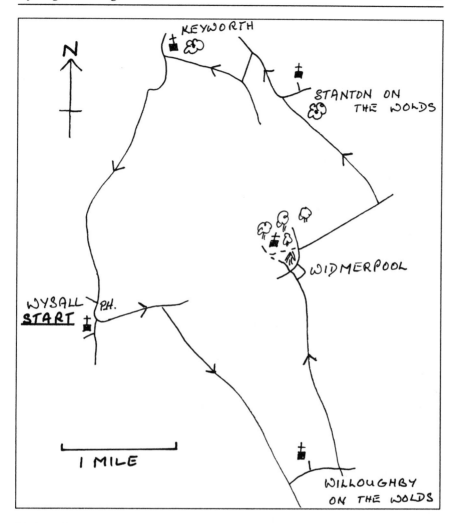

Philip Monckton, were routed by Colonel Rossiter and his men. In the church is a small brass to a Royalist slain in the battle.

Turn left at the crossroads towards the end of the village, signposted to Widmerpool. This road drops quite gently from about 100 metres and as Widmerpool is approached the Gothic Victorian Hall can be seen on the hill above, surrounded by the trees which dominate this lovely village and almost completely hide the church. On reaching the village turn left at the T-junction and immediately turn right into Church Lane. This lane winds a way between impressive country houses, and ends with no sign of a church. Continue along the footpath with no indication that it may lead to the church other than a handsome Cedar towering over the trees ahead. The path crosses a bridge over a small stream and joins a drive. Turn left and take the right fork through the trees to visit the church of St Peter and St Paul in its secret, sheltered glade where two unknown soldiers, slain at Willoughby Field during the Civil War, have their last resting place. The left fork leads to Widmerpool Hall which is not open to the public.

On leaving the church return to the drive turning left and following this private drive out to the road with a stream on your right. On reaching the road go straight over into a lane signposted to Kinoulton, and in about a mile turn left into Thurlby Lane, signposted to Stanton. This is a real Wolds lane, narrow and steep, both down and up; though it is straight, cars can approach silently from behind on windy days and take you by surprise, so take care. There are private gardens occasionally open to the public in both Stanton on the Wolds and nearby Keywoth, consult The National Gardens Scheme leaflet for details.

When Thurlby Lane reaches Stanton on the Wolds it joins a more major road on a bend. The route continues to the left but if you wish to see the tiny All Saints Church, with its 600-year-old window and small 14th century doorway, hidden among trees on the edge of a golf course with views across the Trent Valley, you need to turn right and first left.

Returning to the route the road runs between post-war houses. Take the first turning on the left, signposted to Keyworth and called Willow Brook. On the right are some well-tended Allotment Gardens each with a huge heap of stable manure. It is easy to see that you are in horse country. When you reach the church of St Mary Magdalene, turn left onto the main street of Keyworth. The 14th century tower of the church, visible for miles around, was used in years gone by as a signalling station linking Nottingham, Belvoir Castle, and Charnwood Forest. You may be more interested in the Inn, or the Bakery Tea Shop on the main road. A little further along the road there is a handsome timber frame barn on the left with beautiful herringbone brickwork.

The road bends sharp right, sharp left, then begins a long, sweeping descent. Of course there is a price to pay, but the climb is helped by a few wiggles in the road and before you know it you are on the top of the world again with folds of the beautiful Wolds all around. After passing Longcliffe Farm watch out for the medieval ridge and furrow in the fields on your left. The road now runs down into Wysall and the end of the ride.

31. Bunny
– Home of the Wrestling Baronet

Distance: 10 miles

Route: Wysall – Bunny – East Leake – Wysall

Surface: Tarmac

Start: Wysall (SK604273)

Map: O.S. Landranger 129

Parking: Limited in the village. Ask permission at The Plough.

Accommodation: For camping try: Brooklea Farm, Wysall, Tel. 01509 880792. This is a small farm site. Contact Nottingham County Council, Tel. 0115 977 4212, for details of other accommodation.

Comment: This ride is less strenuous than the previous one, though it does include a gentle climb and a glorious swoop down. The route is all on tarmac, mostly minor lanes but a very short section on the busy, fast, and narrow A60. The village of Bunny was the family home of Sir Thomas Parkyns, born 1663, who collected stone coffins, wrote a book about wrestling, and displayed his love of Latin by displaying Latin quotations all over his estate.

The Journey

The ride starts in the village of Wysall from the car park of The Plough, as the previous ride does. This time, turn left out of the car park and immediately begin to climb. Take the first turning on the left, signposted to Bunny, and continue the gentle climb from just under 80 metres to a little over 90 metres in about three quarters of a mile. After passing Lodge Farm on your left the lane begins a great swoop down Windmill Hill, through Old Wood, to a height of around 40 metres. Take the first turning on the left, opposite a farm, along an even narrower lane 'Unsuitable for Heavy Goods Vehicles', that wanders along with the stream known as Faitham Brook on your right. Beyond the stream you will see the remains of a decaying brick wall. This is part of the three-mile wall around Sir Thomas Parkyn's estate.

On reaching the A60 turn right and cycle into the village of Bunny, taking the first turning left which will take you into the village and off the A60. There is a post office and general store on the left opposite St Mary's Church which holds many monuments to the Parkyn family including a life-size figure of the wrestling Baronet himself ready for a wrestling bout. Beside

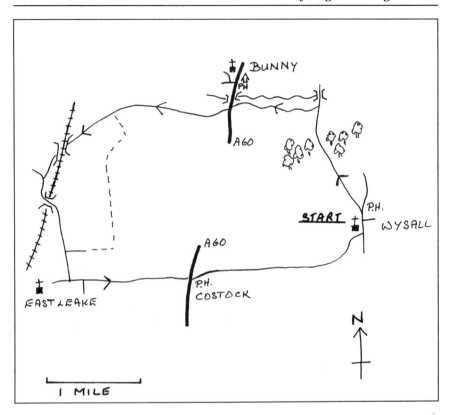

him lays a tiny figure of him defeated by death. Outside the church gates is the school that he built, bearing not only the date of 1700 but a Latin quotation. On the far side of the A60 stands Bunny Hall behind a high brick wall. The Hall, which includes some very odd architecture, is in a sad state of repair but a builder is developing the stables, barns, laundry, etc., into high class housing and hopefully will also restore the house.

From the lane by the church turn right onto the A60, opposite The Rancliffe Arms. Cycle with care for about a quarter of a mile, then turn first right into Gotham Lane, signposted to East Leake. This is a gently undulating lane with a steep hill on your left and the Faitham Brook on the right.

Optional diversion:

Continue to East Leake by road but for those looking for a challenge there is an off-road route into East Leake. If your group decides to split up here it might be a good idea to arrange to re-group at the church in East Leake. Just

Bunny Hall

after passing Welldale Farm on your right there is a signed bridle-path on the left which crosses the field, climbs steeply up to the top of the hill then drops down into East Leake, rejoining the main route beside the school. This would turn a gentle ride into a hard one.

Main route:

Continue along the road past Welldale Farm, passing under the railway bridge and turn left at the T-junction, which is more of a bend and signposted to East Leake. The road climbs abruptly, crosses over the railway and runs into East Leake. There is a service road running parallel on the left which would be useful if the road is busy. Soon the route passes the school on your left where those using the diversion will eventually rejoin the route. When the road reaches a T-junction with the National Westminster Bank ahead, the route turns left but the church, which includes some fine herringbone masonry, and shops are to the right.

After turning left by the Bank, continue straight on to the A60. Cross straight over with the Red Lion ahead, into Wysall Lane. The road continues, still almost flat until it makes a short climb into Wysall.

The Trent Valley

The following two rides form a two-day circular route from Newark along the south of the River Trent to Nottingham then returning along the north of the river to Newark. They also link with a Lincolnshire ride from Newark to Lincoln City. The route was intended to follow bridle-paths along the river-side from Newark town centre to the village of Farndon. However, the bridle-paths are obstructed with barbed wire and stiles as they have been demoted to footpaths. This is a reminder that the presence of a bridle-path on even the O.S. maps does not mean that it still exists. The road alternatives lead to several crossings of the A46. Therefore we cannot recommend this route for young families, though most of the riding is on quiet country lanes or bridle-paths.

The bridle-paths on the route along the north of the river, from Nottingham towards Newark, are good. Access to Newark from the north west is poor for cyclists, all routes entailing considerable distances on narrow and busy main roads. We have therefore suggested alternative options for the end of the journey.

32. Newark to Nottingham – south of the Trent Valley

Distance:	25.5 miles
Route:	Newark – Hawton – Farndon – Thorpe – East Stoke – Elston – Sibthorpe – Flintham – Kneeton – East Bridgford – Shelford – Radcliffe on Trent – Holme Pierrepont
Surface:	Tarmac; one short section of dirt bridle-path
Start:	Either Newark Station (SK805545), or Trent Lock Car Park Newark (SK796541), or Farndon (SK521769)
Map:	O.S. Landranger 120 & 129, also District of Newark & Sherwood Official Map.
Parking:	Either Trent Lock Car Park, Newark; or The Lazy Otter, Farndon.
Accommodation:	There is a wide variety of accommodation available in Newark, contact Newark & Sherwood Tourist Centre, Tel. 01636 78962. For camping contact The Lazy Otter, Farndon, Tel. 01636 702416. Also Holme Pierrepont caravan & camping park, Tel. 0115 982 1212.
Comment:	Newark is a lovely historic market town which was a Royalist stronghold at the time of the Civil War. Those travelling by car or train may wish to spend a day around the town before setting off on the sinuous journey to Nottingham. The route is not flat as it cannot follow the river bank, but snakes along between the river and the Vale of Belvoir. However, the few hills are short and sharp. The one bridle-path may be rough, but again is short, though it leads to a short, very steep, stony track. The ride ends at Holme Pierrepont, the National Water Sports Centre, another good place to spend a day; for details of current events, Tel. 0115 982 1212

The Journey

There are two railway stations in Newark, for those arriving at Newark Castle Station turn left onto the A6065. Shortly, on the right, is Trent Lock Long Stay Car Park, the best car park for those arriving by car. They should turn right onto the A6065 and cross the bridge over the River Trent with the rail travellers. On the right are the ruins of Newark Castle which Cromwell ordered the people of Newark to destroy after the Civil War but fortunately

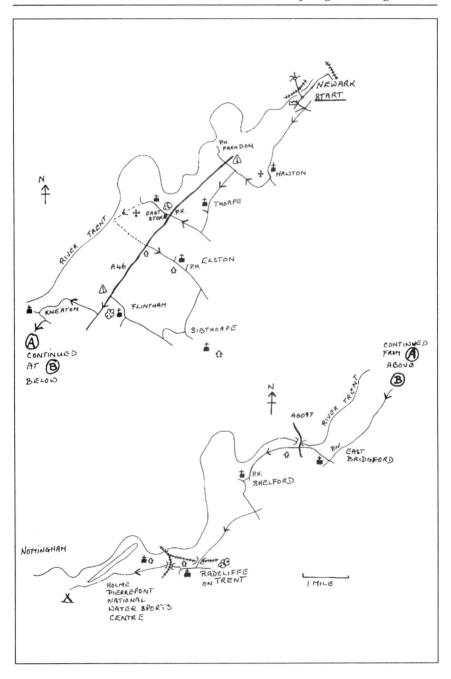

they were very slow workers and the job was never completed. At the roundabout ahead the route is joined by those who arrived by trains stopping at Northgate Station, and on the left here is Newark's Tourist Office.

Arrivals at Northgate Station should turn left along Lincoln Street and Appleton Gate, right into Queen's Road and then left into North Gate and join the route at the roundabout.

From the roundabout continue along Castle Gate with the castle on your right. The road swings sharp left into Lombard Street. At the next junction, when the road swings right, immediately take the left-hand fork, Albert Street, with a church on your left. At the crossroads with Boundary Road keep straight on into Hawton Road. Stay with this road as it runs out of Newark, with the Queens Sconce a famous fortification of the Civil War, to the right, and continue to Hawton. Here there is a church with a chancel built in 1325 by Sir Robert de Crompton, and a tower dating from the 1400s built by Sir Thomas Molineux, the two major local families.

Turn right just beyond the church, signposted to Farndon, and follow the lane as it crosses the River Devon, where there is the site of another Civil War fort to your right, and continues in a north westerly direction towards the Fosse Way (A46). About a quarter of a mile short of the A46 take the left turn signposted to Thorpe. This is where those who have camped at Farndon will join the route.

The Start for those who choose to camp at Farndon.

The Lazy Otter Inn stands at the end of Wyke Lane, Farndon, on the bank of the River Trent. Beside it is a restaurant and nearby a general store. There was a ferry across the Trent here but it is now defunct. There is fishing along the banks of the river and a couple of sailing clubs nearby. The Inn has a large grassed area beside the river, used as a picnic spot, a car park, and for occasional camping. There are toilets but no washing facilities.

From the Inn take Wyke Lane to the left and uphill slightly, turn right into Marsh Lane with the general store on your left. Turn left at the next junction into Main Street when you will have another pub and the Post Office on your right. Cross straight over the A46. Hardy's Farm Shop is on your left shortly. Continue along this lane and take the first turning on the right, signposted to Thorpe. You have now joined the route from Newark.

Main route

The route now continues to the village of Thorpe whose lord of the manor,

Sir William de Thorpe, took part in the battle of Crecy, in 1346, when Edward III's hugely outnumbered army defeated the French army of Philip VI. The French attacked at sunset, confident of victory, but the English archers' arrows flew so thick and fast, 'that it seemed snow', and before midnight a wall of slain French lay before the English lines and Philip fled.

An effigy of Sir William de Thorpe's widow lies in the church of St Lawrence, which stands on the right of the road. Keep straight on through Thorpe to a T-junction. Turn right, signposted to East Stoke. You will reach the A46 with the Pauncefote Arms on your right. Baron Julian Pauncefote, whose family home was East Stoke, was the first Ambassador to the United States. Cross straight over and continue with the wall and tall trees of Stoke Hall Estate (dating from the mid-16th century) on your right. Pass under a brick arch or bridge, which crosses from the estate on your right to the walled garden on the left, then immediately on your right is the church of St Oswald, which has a lovely tower and a surprisingly bright interior. In the churchyard there is a monument to Baron Julian Pauncefote who died in Washington in 1902.

East Stoke was one of the many villages that suffered badly from the effects of the plague in the 17th century. The normal number of deaths from all causes each year was ten. In 1646 between May and December 158 villagers died of the plague alone, whole families were wiped out. Many more were slain at East Stoke one day in 1487 when Henry VII's army defeated John de la Pole, Earl of Lincoln, and the pretender to the throne Lambert Simnel, who claimed to be the Earl of Warwick. Follow the lane past the church until it bends sharp right. Take the grass track which continues straight ahead and passes along the bottom face of the woods until you eventually pass the site of the battle.

King Henry and his hastily-assembled army marched from Radcliffe on Trent, possibly along the route you follow, on 16th June 1487, to face an army of 7000 which included 2000 German mercenaries and many Irish. The track you are following climbs steeply and in the wood on your left can be seen a deep gash in the hillside. This is known as Red Gutter and is reputedly the place where Henry trapped the bulk of the opposing army during a short three-hour battle and slew so many that the blood ran downhill to turn the Trent red. The Earl of Lincoln was killed but Lambert Simnel became a turn-spit in the royal kitchens.

The track becomes a bridle-path when you reach Red Gutter and angles right across the field below the wood, dropping downhill towards the far hedge. This bridle-path has been left as a green unploughed strip across the field. At the hedge, it has become completely overgrown and you must turn left and follow the edge of the field as best you can with the hedge on your right and beyond that the River Trent until you reach the base of a stony track. Here there are two islands in the river with a weir and a lock on their far side. On the opposite bank, but completely out of sight, is the site of Hazelford Ferry – now defunct. This area is a popular fishing spot and there should be a bridle-path along the banks of the river from the fishermen's car park but the gate is padlocked. It seems the bridle-paths on the south of the river have all been lost.

Instead, take the steep stony track which climbs the hill out of the river valley. As you climb, the site of Stoke Battlefield lies across the fields to your left, just above Stoke Wood. When you reach The Fosse Way (A46), again, cross straight over, signposted to Elston and with the unusual Coeur de Lion restaurant on your right. On the O.S. map this is shown as Elston Towers and on the gate posts is yet another name almost obliterated by cream paint.

The route is now running south east towards the Vale of Belvoir and Belvoir Castle can be seen crowning the far hills. Keep straight on when you reach the village of Elston with the family home of the Darwins on your right at the first road junction. Continuing along the road, catch several glimpses of this handsome mansion before reaching the church, on your left and a row of almshouses on the right built by Ann Darwin in the 18th century. (For details of Elston and the Darwins see Ride 28.) As you leave the village there is a converted windmill on the right.

Take the first right turning after Elston, signposted to Sibthorpe, and as the village of Sibthorpe comes into view watch for the large Dovecote which stands 60ft high and has nesting places for 1,260 birds. Take the first right turn as you reach Sibthorpe, signposted to Flintham, and right again at the T-junction, still for Flintham. From Elston to Flintham you are following part of the route of Ride 28. In Flintham, follow the signs for Newark and stay on the main road through the village, passing the church and Flintham Hall on your left before you again reach the A46.

Here there is no alternative but to turn left along the A46 for about half a mile. There is a path on the left for the first part and when you eventually have to cycle on the road it is about a quarter of a mile downhill to the turning to the right to Kneaton. This is a dangerous road and we suggest pulling onto the verge on your left and waiting for a safe moment to cross rather than waiting in the middle of the road.

Once across the main road the lane is quiet and narrow. Unseen to the right is an airfield and on a good day silent gliders drift with the clouds above this 200ft ridge along the Trent Hills. Kneeton village is very small with only a few red-brick houses and farms. If you turn right opposite the red telephone box in the centre you can visit the church of St Helen, most of which was rebuilt towards the end of the 19th century, but most of the tower dates from about 1500. Behind the church is a farmyard with an extremely handsome barn partly brick and partly timbered. Returning to the centre of the village bear right at the phone box, and right again at the next junction, signposted to East Bridgford.

East Bridgford is a far more substantial village, and about half a mile south, at the junction of the A46 and the A6097 lies the seven-acre site of the Roman Town of Margidunum. Finds made here are now housed in Nottingham and the site can only be approached by the main road. Turn right, signposted to Gunthorpe, just after the Reindeer Inn and before the church of St Peter, and cycle down Cuttle Hill to the banks of the Trent. The lane runs beside the river to a crossroads with the A6097, continue straight over, signposted to Shelford.

The road continues beside the river for a short while before swinging inland as the Trent makes one of its huge meandering loops. On the left of the lane is Shelford Manor, home of the Royalist Stanhope family from 1537 until 1645. In that year the well-fortified manor was attacked by the Roundhead Major-General Poyntz and 2,000 men. They found a weak spot in the defences and breaking-in slaughtered the 140 defenders, including Philip Stanhope, before burning the manor to the ground. The manor was rebuilt in 1676.

In the village of Shelford, turn right into Church Lane just after The Earl of Chesterfield Arms and the church of St Peter and St Paul is on the right towards the end of the lane. Here there are memorials to the Stanhope family. Beyond the church turn left into West Street, signposted to Radcliffe. Now, make the final climb up from the river valley, a steep pull up Malkin Hill to a crossroads. Turn right and follow the undulating road into Radcliffe on Trent. On the far side of the Trent are Nottingham's suburbs.

After crossing a railway bridge turn right onto Radcliffe's main street, signposted to Nottingham, and continue along the road past the church of St Mary which only dates from 1879. The original church, which Henry VII attended before marching to the battle of East Stoke, once housed an oak effigy of Stephen de Radcliffe (1245). A local story tells of the villagers' excitement over a victory over France, a great bonfire was built. Stephen's effigy was dressed to represent Napoleon and burnt at the stake.

Just after the church and almost opposite is a handsome red-brick Manor

House. Continue along the road as far as the bus or coach depot. Turn right opposite here into The Green, a 'No Through' road. Stay on this lane as it swings round behind modern houses and becomes a Private Road with 'Sleeping Policemen' and then a gated track (we have never found the gates closed). Across the fields on the right is the magnificent Elizabethan brick Manor House of Holme Pierrepont. The entrance drive on the right also leads to the church of St Edmund, rebuilt in the late 17th century by the Marquis of Dorchester.

The route continues along the lane, past the entrance to church and Manor House, past the entrance to The National Water Sports Centre on the right, to Holme Pierrepont campsite and the end of the journey.

For those who prefer to end the ride in Nottingham City there are signed cycle routes from Holme Pierrepont into the city where there is a wide variety of accommodation available and access to the railway station.

The ruins of Newark Castle

33. Nottingham to Newark –
the northern bank of the River Trent

Distance: 25 miles

Route: Holme Pierrepont – Adbolton – Colwick – Netherfield –
                       Stoke Bardolph – Burton Joyce – Gunthorpe –
                       Hoveringham – Fiskerton – Rolleston – Kelham –
                       Newark

Surface: Tarmac; dirt & grass bridle-paths, some compacted
                       tracks.

Start: Holme Pierrepont (SK605383) or Colwick Country Park
                       (SK603392)

Map: O.S. Landranger 129 & 120; also The Greater
                       Nottingham Cycle Route Network map, from Tourist
                       Offices.

Parking: Colwick Country Park (SK603392) for those starting the
                       two-day journey from Nottingham.

Accommodation: Wide variety available in Nottingham, Tel. 0115 947 0661
                   for details, and for the Newark area, Tel. 01636 78962.
                   For camping at Brinkley, Tel. 01636 812257, for camping
                   at Cromwell, Tel. 01636 821224. For A1 Campsite, North
                   Muskham, Tel. 01636 76558. Also Holme Pierrepont
                   caravan & camping park, Tel. 0115 982 1212.

Comment: We have started this ride from Holme Pierrepont to
                       complete the circle begun with the previous ride, but it is
                       easy to pick up the route from Nottingham City at Colwick
                       Country Park by following the signed City Cycle Routes.
                       The end of the ride is more problematical. You may
                       choose to end the ride at Rolleston, the Kate Greenaway
                       village, and camp at nearby Brinkley, thus linking with the
                       Southwell rides. Alternatively, continue to Kelham and
                       north to camp at Cromwell, or south from South
                       Muskham into Newark. Whichever you decide, you will
                       enjoy the ride along the north bank of the Trent. It is a
                       shame that none of the ferries are still operating as they
                       would add an interesting dimension to these two rides.

The Journey

From Holme Pierrepont campsite turn left onto the road, there is a cycle path
on the right of the road. Turn right at sign Adbolton Lane and immediately

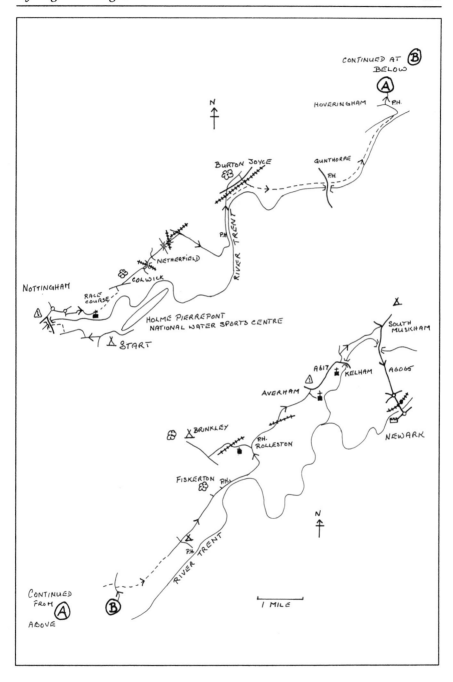

left into a road with a sign for 'Cheshire Homes'. Watch for the blue 'Cycle Route' signs and turn right into Adbolton Grove, signed 'Meadows & City Centre'. These are on road routes but the next turns right across a recreation area just before Melbourne Road, and is again signed Meadows etc. The path swings left on reaching the river and passes under Lady Bay Bridge. Those who feel strong enough can carry their bikes up the steps, on the left, onto Lady Bay Bridge. The rest of us can continue to the Football Ground, turn left and cycle through two car parks, keeping left, cross a road, take a path through a hedge and turn left onto the pavement beside the road over Lady Bay Bridge. This is not an official cycle route, though the locals use it, and if busy you should walk.

At the traffic lights turn right into Meadow Lane. At the roundabout we find the signs extremely confusing. To reach Colwick, you need to turn right into Daleside Road where there is another cycle path on the left of the road. Following the signs, one has to make five traffic-light crossings at this busy junction and take care not to find yourself going back the way you have just come! A more rational route is to stay on the left of the roundabout, cross Manvers Street dual carriageway by the two traffic light crossings and turn right along the Daleside Road cycle path to Colwick.

Take care along this cycle path, factory workers on the left do not necessarily 'think cyclist'. Just before reaching a small roundabout the route crosses Daleside Road and becomes an on-road cycle way on Trent Lane. Almost immediately turn left into Little Tennis Street, signed Colwick Country Park cycle route. At the T-junction, unsigned, turn left and take a narrow path, signed, on the right of Bancrofts' building. This leads to a road around the Race Course, turn right and continue to Colwick Hall.

The Hall, built in 1776 and now a hotel, stands on the site of a mill listed in the Domesday Book of 1086, which also mentions a church. Later, the estate was held by the De Colwicks for a rent of 12 barbed arrows. Colwick Hall was once the home of Byron's first love Mary Chaworth of Annesley, who did not return his love and married John Muster, the sporting squire of Colwick. The church, which stands beside the hotel, is now just a shell but there are still stones commemorating some of the families related to the place, including a Strelly.

On your left is Colwick Race Course and you pass Colwick Hall, which has a grandstand view, continuing to a car park. This is where those starting from Nottingham officially join the route.

Cycle through the car park and take the cinder path at the far end, still with the race track on your left. Follow straight ahead through trees and

Stable block in Kelham village

shrubs, until you reach a clearing which has a Fitness Course. Can you ring the bell? Take the track ahead that climbs a bank and runs behind an estate of flat-roofed houses. Turn left onto a track just beyond the houses and cycle along the estate service road, with the houses still on your left, until you can turn right to a busy road. Cross straight over, with care, to a cycle-path and turn right. On your left is a caravan sales firm. Continue to a road junction and branch left, signed with the blue cycle route symbol to Netherfields and with a car showroom on your left. The route is now an on-road route through a residential area.

Follow the road as it bends sharp right and then turn left onto Claworth Road which climbs steeply to bridge a railway before dropping down to the centre of Netherfields. Just before reaching a small roundabout get off your bike and cross the pelican crossing to the right of the road, then left across another crossing to a 'No Entry' road, Chandos Street. This is a good place to do some shopping.

Continuing, walk along Chandos Street to a crossroads, perhaps a hundred yards, when you can cycle again continuing straight ahead between the houses. The road becomes smaller, passes under a road bridge and then reaches a T-junction with a level crossing to the left. Turn right and head for Stoke Bardolph with a large sewage works on your left. Now at last you have left the town behind.

The road runs towards the River Trent where Stoke Bardolph stands on this northern bank. Today it is a tiny estate village but in 1086 there were a church and two mills here. The road swings left and continues with the river close on the right towards Burton Joyce. Just before reaching a level crossing there is a new track on the right which has a sign saying 'Estate Vehicles Only'. For those who have no wish to visit Burton Joyce this is a short cut which avoids crossing the A612 twice.

There are several gardens open to the public on various occasions in Burton Joyce, see the National Gardens Scheme leaflet, plus several small shops. To reach the village cross the level crossing and straight over the A612 into the main village street. To continue the journey, take the third turning on the right, Meadow Lane, with a Methodist Chapel on the corner. Again cross straight over the A612 into a tiny lane. At the almost unused level crossing cross straight over onto a track and straight over a crossroads of tracks. This is where those who took the short cut rejoin the route turning right at the cross tracks.

This track passes some allotment gardens on your left then reaches the river where it bears left and shortly crosses one of the Trent's loops along a hedged track. Keep straight ahead along a good track which becomes a quite narrow, but good, bridle-path, until you reach the A6097. Cross straight over (public toilets on the left) and down the slope to The Unicorn which stands on the river bank at Gunthorpe.

On the opposite bank is the road from East Bridgford to Shelford that you cycled along on the Newark to Nottingham ride. Follow the lane past The Unicorn to Gunthorpe Lock then through the pair of white gates and continue along the river bank, keeping to the path on the left. The fields on the left have no fences between them and the river and the cattle there are accustomed to people and cycles passing through their territory, showing no interest at all. The farmer concerned obviously does not feel the same benevolence towards the public, and on several gates you will pass through along this bridle-path are signs, written in blood red, warning of the presence of a bull. We did not see any along the route.

The going is good for a grass path, the scenery is beautiful, gates are easy and it is impossible to get lost with the wide reaches of the beautiful Trent curling along silently beside you. You may be greeted by a dog taking his owner for a walk or a fisherman wondering who is disturbing the birds which drift lazily overhead telling the world that you are there. The feeling of warm peace in this bowl of land protected from the southerly winds by the steep hills on the south bank, is a great experience.

The path eventually joins a lane, which has been running parallel for a quarter of a mile, which shortly swings left and runs into the village of Hoveringham. Bear right through the village passing the Marquis of Granby and The Reindeer before heading out of the village into open countryside again where you are going to take a bridle-path on the right. Watch carefully for a tiny stream that passes under the road, just beyond it the bridle-path sign is almost hidden by growing trees and shrubs. If you reach a clear bridle-path sign on your left you have gone too far.

The path swings right around the shrubs and trees with the field on your left, until it reaches the banks of the tiny stream which it follows before swinging left to a track that crosses at right angles on its way to the gravel pits on your right. Cross this track, over the bridge beyond which crosses the conveyor belt for the gravel, and through a gate into another field. Continue straight ahead with the hedge on your right. Watch out for huge blue arrow signs. Across the field the path joins a track which crosses a drain and continues ahead.

Through a gate the bridle-path seems to disappear, the gate on the right bears a Private notice, but almost hidden in an exuberant hawthorn is a small snicket gate with a blue arrow sign. Go through the gate and keep left towards a large gate out onto a lane with Glebe Farm and buildings on your right.

Continue along this lane through the tiny hamlet of Gibsmere to a crossroads. On the far right-hand corner is a Camping & Caravanning Club camp site and down the lane on the right is The Hazelford Ferry Hotel, a very pleasant place for a meal, but without a ferry crossing. The route crosses straight over the crossroads, signposted to Fiskerton. Follow the road to Fiskerton a popular fishing place on the River Trent with views across the river to Red Gutter where Henry VII's army destroyed the Yorkists attempt to put Lambert Simnel on the throne. Many soldiers who survived the slaughter tried to swim across the Trent to Fiskerton most drowning in the attempt.

Beyond Fiskerton the road swings inland again to the village of Rolleston. Once home of the Neville family, this village is now better known as the childhood home of Kate Greenaway who drew lovely pictures of Victorian children to illustrate her books.

This is the place where you can make your first choice about the end of your journey. If you wish to link this ride with the Southwell rides rather than continuing to Newark: turn left in the centre of Rolleston and cycle past the church; go over the level crossing and pass the entrance to Southwell Race Course; turn right at Fiskerton Station and end the journey at The Orchards campsite, Brinkley.

For those who are continuing with the ride, cycle straight through Rolleston to Averham (pronounced 'Airam'), passing along the way a power station which has intruded into the distant views for some time. Averham was the home of the Suttons back in the 13th century but their old Manor House was destroyed by Cromwell. The family name became Manners-Sutton and different members have been Archbishop of Canterbury, Lord Chancellor of Ireland, Speaker of the House of Commons and Ambassador to Spain. The village is probably known best today as the home of The Robin Hood Theatre.

In 1912 the rector of Averham, Reverend Joseph Cyril Walker, built a small theatre in the grounds of the Rectory where he produced musicals for the local population. He timed the shows to coincide with the full moon so that the audience might find their way easily. For a few years the theatre was closed by fire regulations but is now open again. Tel. 01636 706097 for details.

At Averham the route turns right onto the A617. This is the main road from Mansfield and Derbyshire and is very busy, though there is a pavement. The road runs into Kelham, another home of the Manners-Sutton family and there is a magnificent stable block on the right where the road also bends right. In a few yards turn left onto a minor road, signposted to Muskham and shortly afterwards, take the right fork to Muskham.

In South Muskham there are two choices; either cross the main road into the village and follow the signs to either North Muskham camp site or one at Cromwell.

Or turn right onto the A616 for Newark. This is the old Great North Road but with the A1 sweeping around the area to the east this is now probably the safest route into Newark from the west. Follow the road to a roundabout with the Newark By-pass, take great care here traffic is extremely heavy. Take the second exit off the roundabout – it is probably best to use the marked cycle crossings. Cycle into Newark with Trent Lock Car Park on your right just before the bridge over the Trent, with the remains of Newark Castle on the far side of the river. The Tourist Office is on the left just over the bridge.

Canal
&
River Routes

The next two rides follow the Chesterfield Canal and the River Idle. They
make a two-day circular route that could begin either at Retford or West
Stockwith. As you are following two waterways, the going is relatively
level, but towpath riding can be tiring for both the knees and the wrists as
the going is frequently bumpy. Do stop frequently for refreshments, rest,
and to view the wild life of the canal. For cycling on the towpath a Cycling
Permit is required from British Waterways. In the past this cost three
pounds, but things are changing and in 1994 the permit was free. Do apply
for your permit as this gives the authorities an idea of just how many
people do want to use the traffic-free towpaths.

It is also important to remember that these paths are narrow and used
regularly by walkers and fishermen. Always cycle with care and consideration. Do what you can to improve the image of cyclists generally.

We had intended to make these into a three-day ride from Worksop but
the canal towpath from Worksop to Retford proved highly dangerous in
places. We had to walk in several spots and in another, that seemed not
too bad, Penny cycled straight into the canal when she took her eyes off
the track for a moment! However, there is work going on along this stretch
of the canal and if they improve the towpath there will be an excellent route
all the way from the River Trent, across northern Nottinghamshire, into
Derbyshire. Apart from the accommodation mentioned in the details of
the two rides we suggest there is an excellent camp site, Riverside Caravan
Park (Tel. 01909 474118), in Worksop at the Cricket Ground, right beside
the canal, and the helpful managers, Bob and Hazel Hurst, tell us the path
from Worksop towards Chesterfield is in good condition. For up to date
information on the state of canal and path contact:The Secretary, Chesterfield Canal Society, Tapton Lock Cottage, Lockford Lane, Chesterfield,
Derbyshire, S41 7JB. They also have several good books available on the
Chesterfield Canal. At present there is a good rail connection between
Retford and Worksop.

We recommend travelling from Retford to West Stockwith along the
Chesterfield Canal towpath, and from West Stockwith to Retford along
tracks and lanes beside or near the River Idle. This means that whichever
place you use as your start to the ride you will be travelling anti-clockwise.

34. Retford to West Stockwith along the Chesterfield Canal

Distance:	16 miles
Route:	West Retford – Clarborough – Hayton – Clayworth – Wiseton – Gringley on the Hill – Misterton – West Stockwith
Surface:	Mostly compacted earth
Start:	Cemetery, West Retford (SK695815)
Map:	O.S. Landranger 120 & 112 also O.S. Guide to the Waterways 3: North
Parking:	There are several car parks in the centre of East Retford
Accommodation:	Wide selection of B&B in Retford – for details contact Tourist Information, Retford, Tel 01777 860780. In West Stockwith contact The White Hart Inn, Tel 01427 890176.
Comment:	The entire route is on the tow-path, it is a level ride but quite bumpy in places. Tow-path riding is not advisable for young children as there is never a barrier between path and water, though most of this path is quite wide. A journey along a canal could lack interest for some, perhaps uninterested in birds and wild flowers etc, but there are also often interesting villages close by with fine churches, gardens open to the public, farm walks or nature reserves. Retford is an interesting old town which is worthy of at least a day for exploring.

The Journey

The ride begins at the cemetery, West Retford, on the A638. This cemetery is more like an arboretum and is a very pleasant place for an evening stroll if you are staying close by. Take the main path through the cemetery towards a wrought iron bridge over the canal to the rest of the cemetery. Take the path before the iron bridge, to the left with a park bench on your left. This leads to a gate onto the tow-path, almost under the bridge, which is bridge 54b. Turn left onto the tow-path with the canal on your right. Retford is quite a busy town and you are about to cycle right through the heart of it, yet you hardly see or even hear a vehicle. The canal is flanked through the town by green and open spaces. The trees in the cemetery, on the far side of the canal, are magnificent, and bushes line the path on your left. Going is firm and wide.

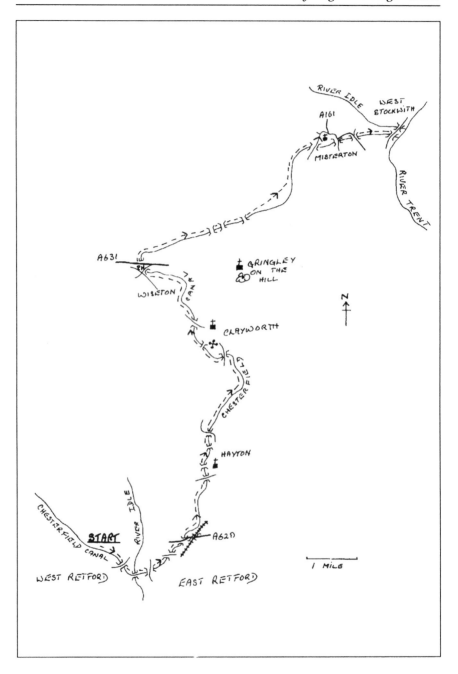

The first lock you reach is West Retford Lock then the path continues, crossing three small aqueducts including one over the River Idle, before reaching Retford Lock the first of the narrow locks. West Retford Lock is over seven feet wide, but Retford Lock is only just over four feet wide and it seems impossible for a boat to pass through. Hopefully there will be some traffic on the canal and you will be able to watch one of the highly decorated narrow boats negotiating one of the seven locks between West Retford and the Trent. Do be careful at locks, watch for the small bollards, only about six inches high, and the rings set into the ground which the boats use for tying-up to, bump into one of those and you could be going for a swim!

The canal twists and bends as it follows a roughly U-shaped course through Retford, passing on the way a large Asda Store car park and several pubs. The bridges all have numbers on them but in the Ordnance Survey Canal Book each bridge is given its name, which is far more romantic. You leave the environs of Retford, passing through grazing land and common land that is undergoing refurbishment. Pass under Clayter's Bridge and Hop Pole Bridge (there is an Inn here serving Real Ale) and reach the next narrow lock, Whitsunday Pie Lock. It appears a local farmer's wife baked a special pie for the navvies building the canal on Whit Sunday, the day they finished building the lock.

The east/west railway line, and the A620 run close to the southern side of the canal at the Whitsunday Pie Lock (the last for about 9 miles). The canal then swings north, away from civilisation and through open countryside with rising land to the east and the broad valley of the River Idle to the west. The village of Clarborough stands on the rising ground to the east with views south west over the canal to Sherwood Forest, and a pub called 'The Gate' close to the bridge known as Clarborough Top Bridge which would give access to Clarborough.

The next village along the route is Hayton, though you see little of it, but if you cross the first bridge you can visit the church of St Peter, a Norman church with an unusual 15th century porch. You pass through Hayton almost without realising it and, after Hayton Low Bridge where there is a canal pub called The Boat Inn, you continue out into open countryside with just the company of the canal wildlife for a stretch of about two miles.

Luckily the butterflies and birds offer plenty of distractions. There is the odd splosh in the water which sets you wondering if it was a giant fish or perhaps Ratty preparing for a day on the river. Some of the fish lazily swimming in secret spots seem to be huge, and in other areas there are shoals of inch long young fish. The path is mostly a wide mown strip of varying quality, with many small pot-holes that would be easier with mountain bikes! On your left there is usually a hedge, frequently covered in brambles, great for blackberrying in the autumn.

Between the path and the canal is a thick swathe of waterside plants, often standing three or more feet tall. Here there will almost always be some plant in flower, and the variety can be quite stunning. Of course the canal is not a natural waterway and often cuts through dry grassland. On one side you may have plants of the dry heathland that normally grow far from water and on the other you have golden water lilies almost hidden by tall clumps probably including yellow flag, water mint, and purple loosestrife. This abundance of wild flowers attracts large numbers of insects. The electric blue of the common damselfly, *Enallagma Cyathigerum*, is obvious as they dart from plant to plant in search of delicate morsels of food such as those dratted midges. If you are lucky one may even join you as you study your insect book, quivering gently like a beautiful jewel on your bar bag. But can you spot an Emperor Dragonfly, or a Darter Dragonfly such as the *Libellula Depressa*? And can you tell the difference?

While you are spotting the water insects take care that you are not running over the butterflies that seem fascinated by the path and love to 'play chicken'. The small tortoiseshell is common, and the red admiral, peacock, and orange-tip are other possibilities. Collins Gem Guides are essential parts of the equipment for this ride.

The route reaches Clayworth Bridge with a Boat Club and turning point for the canal boats. Take special care here watching for the mini bollards and hitching rings. The canal makes a sharp left bend after the bridge, then a right-hand one before reaching Otter's Bridge. This bridge is named after a local family who lived at Royston Manor in the village of Clayworth on the far side of the canal. The next bridge carries a Roman Road over the canal and the route becomes more wooded, though there is nothing dangerous here, unlike a spot on the Worksop to Retford section (which we do not recommend), where a branch was so low it could knock your head off!

The route now approaches Wiseton and the tow-path becomes a tarmac lane for a brief spell before reverting to dirt by Wiseton Top bridge as the canal skirts the estate village of Wiseton, the first place on the route on the same side of the canal as the tow-path. The canal now swings sharp left, away from Gringley on the Hill which crowns the hills on your right. The canal skirts round to the north of Gringley where there is good access to this historic village.

First, the canal plunges into a tunnel under Cuckoo Hill, known as

Drakeholes, and you have to take very briefly to the road. When the canal turns sharp right to enter the tunnel, you can see the other end so it is quite short, cycle onto the road, which is on your left, turning right onto it and cycling up the hill with The Griff Inn on your left and two tiny derelict lodges amongst overgrown shrubs on your right. This is a four-road junction with the A631 close by and it may be busy, so take care. Keep right and aim for an old red brick wall on the left up the hill. Take the track on the left just before the wall, then pass a farm yard on your right before going over a slight rise. Here it is obvious this is an old tarmac road, and under the trees on the left a steep track leads down to the canal where it emerges from the hillside into a leafy green cutting.

The busy A631 crosses high overhead, the canal swings right and you are on your own again. On your own with the birds, bees, cheeky ducks, and shy moorhen chicks, the tall stately herons who trust no-one, and black coots, normally a shy bird, but here behaved as though we did not exist as they stalked across the surface of the water on thick patches of weeds. We did not spot a kingfisher but they are here somewhere, as are the bats which you may spot if evening is approaching.

Gringley Top Lock is about a mile and three quarters from the tunnel and then in quite a short distance there are three bridges over the canal. If you take either the first, Hewitt's Bridge, or the second, Middle Bridge, you can make a short diversion into Gringley on the Hill. Here the church of St Peter and St Paul dates from the 12th century, and on the west side of the village is Beacon Hill, site of an ancient encampment, with views of the surrounding countryside, even as far as Lincoln Cathedral.

Continuing with the ride, you reach Shaw Lock and another bridge over the canal. The tow-path becomes a wide farm track of compacted quarry waste which is a joy to ride on after the pounding of the tow-path. As at most of the road access points to the canal there are many fishermen around here. Then the canal makes a turn to the right. There is a tow-path beside it but we chose to stay on the farm track, which is a bridleway. Continue past Leys Farm to Smith's Bridge, where you rejoin the tow-path down a steep track on the left just before the bridge.

The canal now makes a gentle curve as it heads north towards Misterton with the flat land of the Idle valley on your left and the rising ground of Fountain Hill on the right. Pass two more bridges before reaching the bridge that carries the B1403 over the canal. This is the first access to Misterton. The next section of the tow-path, as it skirts the village, becomes increasingly narrow and overgrown with many nettles. It is not dangerous but we would recommend a diversion into Misterton which has a store, fish and chip shop, pubs and a handsome church.

Leave the tow-path and head north on the B1403. This road runs into the village between old and new housing before reaching the A161. Turn right onto this road which is the main street of the village. On your right is All Saints Church, believed to have existed before 1066 and like most churches parts have been rebuilt at various times in the life of the church, including in 1824 after a major hurricane. The unusual east window, with the prominent hands, feet and heart, was designed by John Piper and made by Patrick Reyntiens in 1965.

The fish and chip shop is on your right as you continue along the main street, with the general store on your left. Stay on the main road until you reach the canal again at the other end of the village. Rejoin the tow-path at Misterton Low Lock, where The Packet Inn serves meals, for the last half mile or so to West Stockwith and the end of the ride.

At West Stockwith there is a mechanised lock which at certain times of the tide can allow the narrow boats access to the River Trent which is tidal almost as far south as Newark. The village is a picturesque spot and was once a thriving port where the canal, the Trent and the then-navigable Idle met. There is a boat yard here, store, pubs and a Miniature World Museum which houses a collection of ancient dolls' houses. Across the river is East Stockwith, Lincolnshire.

Lock on the Chesterfield canal

35. River Idle, the return route from West Stockwith to Retford

Distance: 24 miles plus 3-mile diversion

Route: West Stockwith — Misterton — Misson — Bawtry — Mattersey — Lound — Sutton — West Retford

Surface: Tarmac, dirt tow-path, good farm tracks

Start: West Stockwith (SK786946)

Map: O.S. Landranger 112 & 111

Parking: It should be possible to leave your vehicle in the car park of the Inn providing you are spending at least one night with them. Remember to explain what you are doing.

Accommodation: The White Hart Inn, West Stockwith does B&B; for details phone 01427 890176. There is a wide variety of accommodation in Retford, for details contact the Tourist Office, tel 01777 860780.

Comment: This is a very different ride to the previous one. We have followed the general route rather than sticking close to the river. Much of the ride is on quiet country lanes with one section of main road (which does have a barely used footpath). Most of the going is flat with some hilly bits in the middle. There is an optional diversion to a ruined Priory, and the route also passes a Waterfowl Reserve.

The Journey

Begin the journey by joining the Chesterfield Canal tow-path close to the entrance to The Stockwith Marina. If you have not already visited the marina, spare a moment or two to look at the gaily painted pleasure craft tied up here. The tow-path is on the north of the canal and you will be heading west towards Misterton. Leave the canal at Misterton Low Lock, by the Packet Inn and turn right onto the A161 which will take you through the village. You will not rejoin the canal until right at the end of the ride.

As you cycle through Misterton, you will pass the Post Office and General Store on your right. Continue to the solid grey church of All Saints, and turn left onto the B1403, signposted to Gringley. Pass the Red Hart on your right and round the bend turn right into Church Street, signposted to Cornley. Take the left fork in a hundred yards or so. The land you are cycling through is very flat, it was known as the drowned land at one time, before it was

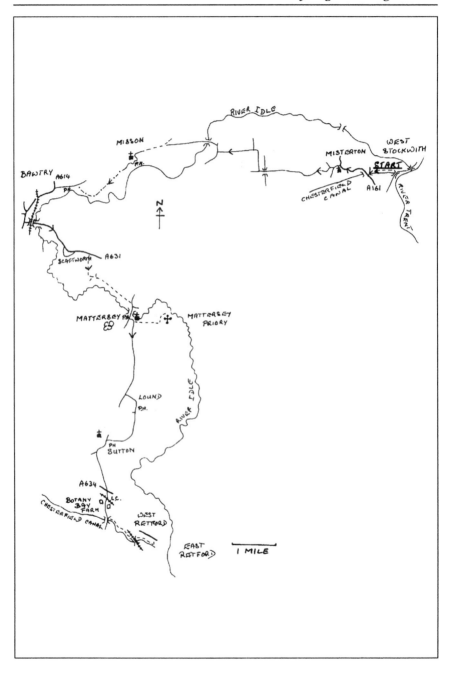

drained and became extremely productive agricultural land. The lane passes virtually through a farm yard, Cattle Farm, with farm buildings on the right and huge static machinery on the left.

Continue straight ahead. The lane crosses a small bridge over a straight drain running at right angles to the lane. Take the next farm track on the right, this is about half a mile from Cattle Farm. You are now using white roads that follow the field edges, sometimes they are reasonable old tarmac, occasionally this is badly broken, and some parts are compacted dirt. Remember to give way to farm vehicles, especially at harvest time. Follow the track as it makes a left turn and continue to a T-junction with a tarmac lane. Turn right and, just before the buildings of North Carr Farm, turn left towards a bridge over the River Idle.

On the far side there is a good track on the left which runs beside the River Idle all the way to Misson. This is a lovely ride with families of swans and other water birds sailing quietly along a broad stretch of remote river used only by fishermen. At the far end of the track is a padlocked gate and a high stile which we do not recommend using though the track would make a pleasant picnic stop. Instead continue straight ahead from the bridge over the river along an unfenced track between arable land. This track widens after a bridle-path joins on the right at an area known as Sand Pit. The old sand pit is on the left, an overgrown area which is home to dozens of rabbits, but there is a notice further on warning of deep water so beware.

The rough track becomes tarmac and on your right is Misson Cemetery. As at most cemeteries, there is a water tap just inside the gate: this one offers the chance to fill your water bottles and is also an interesting old tap. Take the turning on the left, just beyond the cemetery and the 30mph sign, called Gibdyke. Follow the road as it swings right and passes the church and the White Horse Inn. By the church, the lane runs into the main village street, and you continue straight on. When this street bends right and there is a sign for West Street, turn left into Slaynes Lane. This becomes a dirt track as it leaves the village behind and crosses some darker arable land with a drain on the left and, beyond that, the River Idle.

This track continues, swinging right after the second sluice, to the minor road from Misson to Bawtry. Turn left onto this road with the Newington signboard on your left and in a short distance The Ship Inn, which has an excellent children's play area. The name of this Inn may surprise you but the River Idle was at one time a navigable river as far as Bawtry which was quite an important inland port with access, via the Trent, to the greatest transport network in the country. This road is quite narrow and may be a trifle busy but there is a footpath running beside it.

At The Ship Inn the route enters South Yorkshire and in about a quarter of a mile, turn left onto the A614, just after a parade of shops on your left. The A614 is Bawtry's Main Street and great care should be taken as you cycle past parked cars along the busy road as it runs through the wide open centre of this town. A major road joins from the right, the A638, and another, the A631, in the centre of town. In busy towns car occupants can often open the door first and check the road is clear second. A car door swinging open can knock you from your bike or make you swerve into the path of passing cars, don't be bullied by traffic behind you, give the parked cars a wide berth. Bawtry has several pubs and cafes among a wide variety of shops, a good centre for restocking the picnic bags.

Continue straight through the town and down a slight slope to traffic lights. Here turn left onto the A631, signposted to Gainsborough. Round the corner is yet another pub and also some men's loos on the left. The road passes under the railway then crosses the River Idle, where it re-enters Nottinghamshire, before beginning to climb towards Scaftworth. This is a busy main road but there is a footpath. The road becomes a dual-carriage-way, climbs quite a hill, by-passes Scaftworth where the dual-carriageway ends and then begins to drop downhill slightly with the woods on top of Barrow Hills on your left. Watch for the track to Stone Hill Farm on your right. Take this track which drops down from the road, then climbs steeply towards woods and Stone Hill Farm. The soil here is very sandy and in dry seasons parts of the track may be treacherous, take care.

As the track climbs towards Stone Hill Farm between hawthorn hedges you become aware that there are free-range pigs in the field on your left! Turn left onto the track that runs above their field and note how contented they all look. The track continues on a parallel line to the River Idle, which is amongst the trees across the field on your right. Keep straight ahead ignoring all side tracks. The track has a grass strip down the centre which mostly makes good firm riding but the two wheel ruts are often very sandy.

On reaching a minor tarmac road, turn right. This road becomes the B6045 at the first road junction, where you keep straight ahead, then it crosses the River Idle before entering the lovely village of Mattersey. Turn left at the first junction and pass a shop and Post Office, the Barley Mow Inn, and the church of All Saints. This church is worth a short visit, it has several odd gargoyles and is also the home of a colony of bats which, according to a newspaper report, is driving the vicar and parishioners batty!

Just beyond the church the road swings right, but on this bend is the start of a three-mile detour to visit the remains of Mattersey Priory. The Gilbertine Priory, the only English Monastic Order, stands in a curve of the River Idle to the east of Mattersey together with a farmhouse built mainly of stone from the ruined Priory. The track from Mattersey is teeth-rattlingly stony, with an almost imperceptible slope towards the Priory, but the site of the Priory is beautifully maintained by English Heritage. It is easy to see why this spot was chosen by the monks, the ruins stand on a slight rise with the river curving gently around the north and eastern sides and surrounded by an area that must have been extremely boggy land before the drains were dug but was also probably excellent grazing land. The place is very peaceful, another perfect spot for a picnic.

The plaque at Botany Bay level crossing

Returning to the village of Mattersey turn left onto the road again, signposted to Sutton cum Lound. The minor road out of the village is wide and quiet with wide views on either side. It rises fairly gently and on your left is tree-clad Blaco Hill which looks like an ancient Barrow (burial mound). Take the first turning on the left, signposted to Lound, after the farm lane up to Blaco Hill. There is a pleasant hostelry on your left as you pass through this tiny village. Just after the pub there is a crossroads; continue straight on but take care as many heavy trucks cross the road here. Beyond the village the road bends sharp right, on the left here is the entrance to The Wetlands Waterfowl Reserve and Exotic Bird Park. The 32 acre Reserve has a cafe and about 100 different species of birds and animals, some rare breeds.

The route continues into Sutton, where there is a pub and a campsite. Carry on through the village, keeping left at the junction just as you leave Sutton. Cross straight over the A638 and take care as the junction is rather off-set. Cross the railway at the Botany Bay Farm level crossing and continue until you reach the bridge over the Chesterfield Canal. Take the track on the left to join the tow-path on the north bank with the canal on your right. You are now heading south east for Retford and will follow the canal all the way to Retford Cemetery. The path is good but this area is very popular with fishermen, take care and be polite. There are many waterbirds on the canal, butterflies, dragonflies and damselflies, along the tow-path.

You have joined the canal at Lady Bridge, you then pass under the railway bridge before coming to Bridge 54, a handsome iron bridge. Pass through the wrought iron gate on the left, just beyond the bridge, and cycle with care through what appears to be an arboretum but is in fact a lovely, peaceful cemetery. The path will take you out to the A638 in West Retford, East Retford and the Tourist Office is to the right.

36. Clumber Park to Lincoln

Distance: 32 miles direct; 18 & 16 miles if camping at Laneham.

Route: Clumber – Bothamsall – Gamston – Eaton – Upton – Stokeham – Laneham – Ragnall – Dismantled Railway – Hartsholme Country Park, Lincoln.

Surface: Tarmac, compacted dirt bridle-path, compacted shale farm tracks; off-road section on disused railway track with variable surfaces from good to appalling.

Start: Clumber Park (SK625747) or Hardwick Village (SK638755)

Map: O.S. Landranger 120 & 121

Parking: Clumber Park main car park or a small one in the village of Hardwick.

Accommodation: The Camping & Caravanning Club Site, Clumber Park; Tel. 01909 482303. For Lincoln contact Hartsholme Country Park Camping & Caravanning Site, phone 01502 686264. For camping in Laneham if making this a two-day ride, telephone 01777 228428.

Comment: A route from Clumber Park to Lincoln was proposed several years ago by Sustrans, the charity which creates safe routes for walkers, cyclists, and equestrians. Unfortunately the local authorities failed to provide the necessary finance and the route remains only a paper one. The following route follows Sustrans' proposals where possible and links the two complimentary cycling counties as safely as possible. There are two major obstacles to overcome on this route, one is the notorious A1, the other is the almost un-bridged River Trent. We do not recommend this ride for young children, although all but a mile of the route is on quiet country lanes or tracks.

To cross the River Trent we have used the disused railway track beside Marnham Power Station, thus avoiding the only road bridge and several miles on the narrow, and busy, A57. This is an unofficial route as British Rail wish to keep the right to re-open the railway in the future. This railway track can be followed almost into Lincoln and is the most direct route.

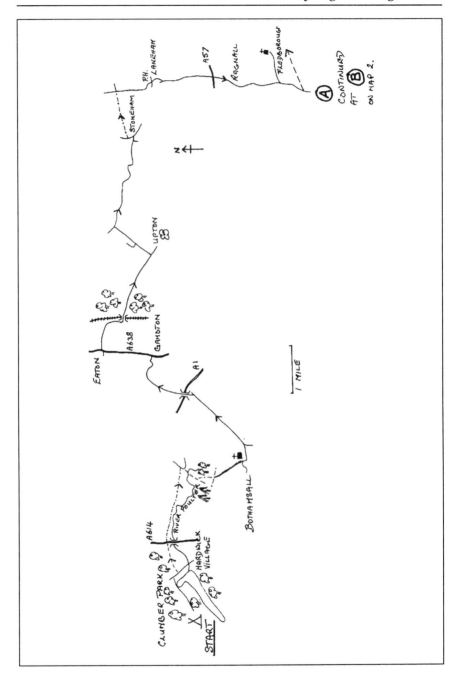

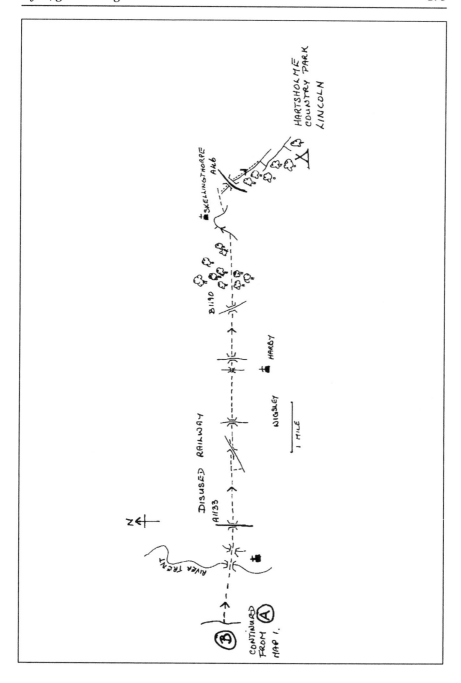

The Journey

The campsite in Clumber Park is in the old walled garden, follow the path beside the lake towards Hardwick Village. Turn left along the footpath past the toilets in the old farm buildings to Hardwick Village Car Park. Follow the track ahead, with farm buildings on your right, to the T-junction with the lane running through the village, turn left. The road climbs slightly and there are one or two speed bumps. Turn right down a dirt farm track, signposted bridle-path, which passes through a 'Pick Your Own' Fruit Farm. The track drops down between fruit and vegetables, then climbs to a gateway. Through the gateway, bear right into a hedged bridleway, though if you wish to buy some fruit for the journey or vegetables for supper, there is a farm shop to the left.

The bridleway goes through a gate onto a tarmac lane and in a few yards, bear right onto a signed bridle-path around the edge of a field. Keep the hedge on your right and on the far side of the field bear right onto a path through a wood, still with the boundary fence on your right. This path will bring you to the A614, a busy, and very fast, bit of straight road. (Sustrans would like to divert the path here to pass under the road a few yards to the south.) Take great care and cross to a narrow gap in the hedge opposite. This narrow path runs along the top of a short hump of land with scratchy gorse crowding in from each side.

The path continues, wider and more pleasant as it leaves the 'A' road behind, through fields and with the River Poulter and its reed beds on your right, watch out for dragon flies and water fowl. The path becomes a good farm track and passes Crookford Farm before reaching a tarmac lane. (Here Sustrans preferred route bears north but at present there is no safe way to cross the A1.) Turn right onto the tarmac lane and cycle downhill to a ford across the River Poulter. This very short section, from the farm track to the bend in the road before the ford, carries heavy trucks which are based at the farm on top of the hill on your left, take care.

Beyond the wide ford, and a footbridge on the right, a stony track climbs the hill through silver birch and then dark, silent conifers. Keep left near the top when a more minor track forks into the main one. Pass through the conifers, then down into arable land before climbing to a bend on a tiny tarmac lane. On joining the lane, keep straight ahead for Bothamsall. In the village, turn left onto another small lane before the church. Continue straight ahead when this becomes a gated bridleway with fields on the left and a wood on your right, until you reach Haughton Park House, on your left. Turn right here and follow the drive down to the road and turn left onto the B6387.

This road bridges the A1 then runs around the edge of Gamston Aero-drome before reaching the A638. Turn left onto this road, there is a narrow pavement on the right, and cycle with great care for just over a mile to Eaton. Turn right here, signposted to East Drayton, onto a minor road that bridges a busy intercity railway line.

There is an alternative way to cross this line which avoids using so much of the 'A' road, but it entails ferrying bike and gear across the tracks. When we first used this route we used the bridle-path across the line but had to make several crossings to carry all our gear over and the trains appeared from nowhere, passing at an appalling speed and with a suction that almost dragged you under them. We have rarely been so terrified in our lives. We only continued with the crossing as there was a track worker there who knew the timetable and told us when we could cross and when to wait. We recommend using the road!

After the road climbs up to cross the railway Eaton Wood, a nature Reserve, is on the left and Gamston Wood on the right, and the route continues downhill to Upton. Take the first turning on the left, signposted to Headon, as you enter the village. The lane crosses a small stream then climbs uphill. Do not take the left turn into Headon, but keep straight on to a T-junction and turn right, signposted to Stokeham. As the lane drops down towards Stokeham the countryside opens out, with distant views to right and left which include water towers of at least two power stations on the Trent and the spires of Lincoln Cathedral.

Stokeham is only a tiny village. Keep straight on through and then turn left at the end of the village, signposted to Treswell. This is the Power Station access road and there may be heavy vehicles, but it has always been quiet when we have used it. In a very short distance there is a dirt track on the right by some trees, turn onto this which varies from very good to just a grass track then back to good again before reaching tarmac once more. (Sustrans proposed route turns left then crosses the River Trent via Torksey railway bridge, but this is impossible at present.) Turn right onto the tarmac lane and continue to Laneham and turn left, signposted to Laneham Ferry.

From here you continue straight ahead if you are planning to make this a two-day ride. Manor House Caravan Site is on your left.

For those continuing to Lincoln, turn first right. There is a weight limit sign and a Post Office on your left. Turn left again at a T-junction onto the power station access road again. Cross straight over the busy A57 taking great care and continue south through the village of Ragnall. In about a mile, when the road you are on turns sharp right, a small lane turns off to the left to Fledborough. Stay on the road, but you may like to make a short diversion to visit the 'Gretna Green' of Nottinghamshire. In the 13th century Fledborough was a busy port on the River Trent, one of the countries main commercial arteries, and in the 1700s Mr Sweetapple, the rector, was prepared to grant marriage licences to anyone.

Returning to the route continue along the road, which is an access road for Marnham Power Station, until you reach two red-brick houses, one on either side of the road, and an old railway bridge. Immediately over the bridge turn left onto a cinder track down to the old railway track.

The track is made of large rough stones where it crosses the River Trent but improves to a reasonable cinder track. There is a steep track down to the first country lane which leads to North and South Clifton, but we recommend staying with the old railway track which runs like an arrow directly towards Lincoln City. The going is good as the track passes under the A1133 and a track to Moor Farm. It passes an old level crossing with a house on your left. On the right a track leads out to a minor road, if you use this take care, the grass strip beside the track is an airstrip!

The track continues under another two roads with access to the second via a green track on the right which gives access to Wigsley. Beyond here the track bridges Wigsley Drain, watch the trees to the right for a sight of the 120ft tall shingle-clad spire of Harby Church. In 1290 Queen Eleanor and Edward I stayed at the Manor House in Harby where Eleanor was taken ill and died. They had been married 36 years and Edward, by many considered to be a hard and treacherous man, mourned the loss of his partner so much he erected a cross in every village that her body rested in on the journey to London for burial. The church now standing in Harby is not the one that stood there in 1290 but it does contain memorials to Eleanor.

To reach Harby, turn left along a cinder track running behind an old railway building beside the track after crossing a second drain and before passing under another road bridge. From this road bridge the going becomes poor, and could be appalling in wet weather as the track crosses the border between Nottinghamshire and Lincolnshire. For those who cannot face pushing the bike, take the track and road to Harby. Continue through the village to Eagle Moor. Turn left and take the left fork at the next junction. Cross straight over the next two crossroads and continue to Skellingthorpe where you should rejoin the off-road riders as they join the road to ride through Skellingthorpe.

For those hardy types who have stayed on the railway track the going is poor, with deep dried ruts in good weather, for nearly a mile. During that mile there is another chance to abort and head for Harby in about a quarter of a mile along a green track that runs back on the right. There is another road bridge with access on the right again, before the bridge, to the B1190 where you can turn right for Doddington which has a magnificent Elizabethan Manor House. Going improves for a quarter of a mile before deteriorating again. As the track enters a wood it improves slightly, there are some blocks of concrete laid across the track but passing is easy for cycles and cycling becomes good again.

There is a factory beyond the field on the right, more blocks across the track and a bridle-path crossing from the right into the woods on the left. Shortly a bog completely blocks the track but walkers and cyclists have made a way past through the shrubs on the left into a dry ditch! Two more bridges cross the track, before the second take the steep cinder path on the left to the top of the embankment and follow to a field track which leads to the road. Turn left and cycle through the village of Skellingthorpe.

This is where those who have aborted along the track and taken to the road should rejoin the route, though there is more off-road riding ahead. There is a By-Pass to negotiate between Skellingthorpe and Lincoln, which was built when no consideration was given to cyclists or foot traffic. It isolates the city's cyclists and walkers, preventing safe access to the surrounding countryside. There is a secret way to avoid this monstrosity.

Take the road through the village of Skellingthorpe, following the signs for Lincoln, and just after the road swings sharp right rejoin the disused railway track on your left. There are concrete blocks and mounds of earth to prevent vehicles getting on to it but access for cycles is easy. Follow the track until it crosses a small drain. Turn right onto a signed path along the bank of the drain, with the drain on your right. These Lincolnshire drains are deep, so don't fall in. Ahead are two stiles which are easily negotiated with empty bikes. If you are carrying heavy panniers you could follow the example of many locals who continue along the railway track to the next gateway on the right and walk around the edge of the field, with the hedge on your right, until you reach the bank of the drain and turn left onto it. This is not an official Right of Way.

The drain passes under the notorious By-Pass. The footpath is routed out onto the road, across this busy and dangerous place, then back down to the drain on the far side. Just how mad can planners get? We, and most other sensible people, continue straight ahead, under the by-pass, which is only handlebar height – but safe.

The footpath continues along the bank of the drain, any track or lane to the right will take you out to Skellingthorpe Road which runs parallel to the drain. We prefer to continue along the path with the drain on your right, until the path crosses to the other bank, close to a pig farm. Here the route turns right and follows the farm track to Skellingthorpe Road. Turn left and continue to Hartsholme Park, on your right, the Caravan Site and the end of the journey.

Access to Lincoln City is straight ahead along Skellingthorpe Road, over the level crossing then turn left onto Tritton Road Cycle Path which will take you into the centre. There is also a good bus service into the centre from Hartsholme.

Lincoln Cathedral

Town & Village Index

A

Adbolton	150
Aslockton	132
Awsworth	66

B

Bawtry	165
Beauvale Priory	60
Bevercotes	109, 115
Bilsthorpe	55
Birklands	11
Bleasby	51
Blidworth	71
Blidworth Wood	71
Blyth	86
Bogend	60
Bothamsall	115, 171
Brinkley	46, 51
Bunny	139
Burton Joyce	150

C

Car Colston	132
Carburton	31, 33, 39
Caunton	83
Clarborough	159
Clayworth	159
Clipston	124
Clipstone Forest	15
Clumber	171
Clumber Park	27, 31
Colston Bassett	120, 124
Colwick	150
Cossall	66
Cossall Marsh	66
Cotgrave	120, 124
Creswell Crags	36
Cropwell Bishop	120, 124
Cropwell Butler	120, 124

E

Eakring	55
East Bridgford	143
East Leake	97, 103, 139
East Markham	109
East Stoke	143
Eastwood	63
Eaton	171
Edwinstowe	11, 14
Elston	128, 143
Epperstone	75

F

Farndon	143
Farnsfield	46, 55
Fiskerton	51, 150
Flintham	128, 143

G

Gamston	171
Gotham	97, 103
Greasley	60
Grimesmoor	75
Gringley on the Hill	159
Gunthorpe	150

H

Halam	46
Hardwick	27, 31
Hawksworth	128, 132
Hawton	143
Hayton	159
Hockerton	83
Hodstock	86
Holbeck Woodhouse	36
Holme Pierrepont	143, 150
Hoveringham	150

K
Kelham   150
Kersall   80
Keyworth   136
KIngston on Soar   97
Kirklington   55
Kneesall   23, 80
Kneeton   143

L
Lambley   75
Laneham   171
Laxton   19 - 20, 23
Lincoln   171
Lound   165
Lowdham   75

M
Maplebeck   80, 83
Mattersey   165
Milton   109, 115
Misson   165
Misterton   159, 165
Moorgreen   60, 63
Morton   51

N
Netherfield   150
Newark   143, 150
Newstead Abbey   74
Norton   39

O
Old Clipstone   11, 14 - 16
Oldcotes   86
Ompton   23
Ossington   20
Owthorpe   120, 124

P
Papplewick Pumping Station   71
Pleasley   91
Pleasley Vale   95

R
Radcliffe on Trent   120, 143
Ragnall   171

Ravenshead   74
Rolleston   150

S
Scarrington   132
Screveton   128, 132
Serlby   86
Shelford   143
Sherwood Forest   11
Sibthorpe   128, 143
Skegby   91
Southwell   46, 51
Stanton on the Wolds   136
Stoke Bardolph   150
Stokeham   171
Stragglethorpe   120, 124
Strelley   66
Styrrup   86
Sutton   165
Sutton Bonington   97

T
Teversal   91
Thoroton   128, 132
Thorpe   143
Thrumpton   97, 103
Thurgarton   51

U
Underwood   63
Upton   171

W
Walesby   115
Watnall   61
Welbeck   39
West Leake   97
West Markham   109, 115
West Retford   159, 165
West Stockwith   159, 165
Westhorpe   51
Widmerpool   136
Willoughby in the Wolds   136
Winkburn   83
Wiseton   159
Woodborough   75
Wysall   136, 139

Cycling Notes

Please use these pages to record any changes to the routes and feel free to send copies to the publisher so that we can maintain an accurate publication.

Cycling Notes

Cycling Notes

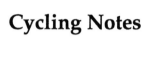

We publish guides to individual towns, plus books on walking and cycling in the great outdoors throughout England and Wales. This is a recent selection:

Cycling . . .

CYCLE UK! The essential guide to leisure cycling – Les Lumsdon *(£9.95)*
OFF-BEAT CYCLING IN THE PEAK DISTRICT – Clive Smith *(£6.95)*
MORE OFF-BEAT CYCLING IN THE PEAK DISTRICT – Clive Smith *(£6.95)*
50 BEST CYCLE RIDES IN CHESHIRE – edited by Graham Beech *(£7.95)*
CYCLING IN THE COTSWOLDS – Stephen Hill *(£6.95)*
CYCLING IN THE CHILTERNS – Henry Tindell *(£7.95)*
CYCLING IN THE LAKE DISTRICT – John Wood *(£7.95)*
CYCLING IN LINCOLNSHIRE – Penny & Bill Howe *(£7.95)*
CYCLING IN STAFFORDSHIRE – Linda Wain *(£7.95)*
CYCLING IN THE WEST COUNTRY – Helen Stephenson *(£7.95)*
CYCLING IN SOUTH WALES – Rosemary Evans *(£7.95)*
CYCLING IN SCOTLAND & N.E.ENGLAND – Philip Routledge *(£7.95)* .
CYCLING IN NORTH WALES – Philip Routledge *(£7.95) ... available 1996*

Country Walking

LAKELAND WALKING: On The Level – Norman Buckley *(£6.95)*
FIFTY CLASSIC WALKS IN THE PENNINES – Terry Marsh *(£8.95)*
HILL WALKS IN MID WALES – Dave Ing *(£8.95)*
WEST PENNINE WALKS – Mike Cresswell *(£5.95)*
WELSH WALKS: Dolgellau /Cambrian Coast – L. Main & M. Perrott *(£5.95)*
WELSH WALKS: Aberystwyth & District – L. Main & M. Perrott *(£5.95)*
WALKS IN MYSTERIOUS WALES – Laurence Main *(£7.95)*
RAMBLES IN NORTH WALES – Roger Redfern *(£6.95)*
RAMBLES AROUND MANCHESTER – Mike Cresswell *(£5.95)*
EAST CHESHIRE WALKS – Graham Beech *(£5.95)*
CHALLENGING WALKS: NW England & N Wales – Ron Astley *(£7.95)*
LONDON BUS-TOP TOURIST – John Wittich *(£6.95)*
TEA SHOP WALKS IN THE CHILTERNS – Jean Patefield *(£6.95)*

BY-WAY TRAVELS SOUTH OF LONDON – Geoff Marshall *(£6.95)*
BY-WAY BIKING IN THE CHILTERNS – Henry Tindell *(£7.95)*
PUB WALKS IN SNOWDONIA – Laurence Main *(£6.95)*
BEST PUB WALKS AROUND CHESTER & THE DEE VALLEY – John Haywood *(£6.95)*
BEST PUB WALKS IN GWENT – Les Lumsdon *(£6.95)*
PUB WALKS IN POWYS – Les Lumsdon & Chris Rushton *(£6.95)*
BEST PUB WALKS IN PEMBROKESHIRE – Laurence Main *(£6.95)*
BEST PUB WALKS AROUND CENTRAL LONDON → Ruth Herman *(£6.95)*
BEST PUB WALKS IN ESSEX – Derek Keeble *(£6.95)*

More Pub Walks . . .

There are many more titles in our fabulous series of 'Pub Walks' books for just about every popular walking area in the UK, all featuring access by public transport. We label our more recent ones as 'best' to differentiate them from inferior competitors!

Explore the Lake District:

THE LAKELAND SUMMITS – Tim Synge *(£7.95)*
100 LAKE DISTRICT HILL WALKS – Gordon Brown *(£7.95)*
LAKELAND ROCKY RAMBLES: Geology beneath your feet – Brian Lynas *(£7.95)*
FULL DAYS ON THE FELLS: Challenging Walks – Adrian Dixon *(£7.95)*
PUB WALKS IN THE LAKE DISTRICT – Neil Coates *(£6.95)*
LAKELAND WALKING, ON THE LEVEL – Norman Buckley *(£6.95)*
MOSTLY DOWNHILL: LEISURELY WALKS, LAKE DISTRICT – Alan Pears *(£6.95)*

Sport . . .

RED FEVER: from Rochdale to Rio as 'United' supporters – Steve Donoghue *(£7.95)*
UNITED WE STOOD: unofficial history of the Ferguson years – Richard Kurt *(£6.95)*
MANCHESTER CITY: Moments to Remember – John Creighton *(£9.95)*

- plus many more entertaining and educational books being regularly added to our list.
All of our books are available from your local bookshop. In case of difficulty, or to obtain our complete catalogue, please contact:

Sigma Leisure, 1 South Oak Lane, Wilmslow, Cheshire SK9 6AR
Phone: 01625 – 531035   Fax: 01625 – 536800

ACCESS and VISA orders welcome – call our friendly sales staff or use our 24 hour Answerphone service! Most orders are despatched on the day we receive your order – you could be enjoying our books in just a couple of days. Please add £2 p&p to all orders.